RUT-BUSTING
BOOK
FOR
WRITERS

RUT-BUSTING
BOOK
FOR
WRITERS

Nancy Christie

MCP - Maitland

Mill City Press, Inc.
2301 Lucien Way #415
Maitland, FL 32751
407.339.4217
www.millcitypress.net

Editor: Ann Henry Literary Services

Quantity sales. Special discounts are available on quantity purchases by corporations, associations, and others. For details, contact Nancy Christie at 330-793-3675 or nancy@nancychristie.com.

Printed in the United States of America

ISBN 13: 978-1-54561-100-5
LCCN: 2017912320

DEDICATION

To all the writers out there—the known and unknown, the published and unpublished, those who share their work and those who keep it private—who write because the urge to express their thoughts and emotions is too strong to be denied.

TABLE OF CONTENTS

PREFACE

The idea for this book grew out of workshops and interviews I have been doing for more than ten years. When my first book, *The Gifts of Change*, came out, I developed my "Rut-Busting" workshop to help people move past their self-imposed restrictions.

From there, it was a natural step to create a "Rut-Busting" workshop specifically for writers since, so often, we tend to fall into one type of rut or another and need ideas and encouragement to take the leap into the unknown.

At the same time, I was interviewing writers on my blogs, and their insights about living the writing life were so valuable and useful that I knew I wanted to do more than just share them online.

So I wrote this book to pull together all the information I have learned through the years, invited other writers to share their hard-earned knowledge and reached out to industry experts for useful tips and suggestions.

Rut-Busting Book for Writers explores how to push past the boundaries to find new ways to use our writing abilities as well as strategies for dealing with the practical side of being in a creative profession.

Writing is more than just a way of expressing our creativity. For many of us, it's our profession—how we earn a living and pay our bills—and it can be challenging to figure out how to balance both these sides of being a writer.

Add in the other demands and responsibilities we all have, and it's no wonder that we look at other writers and wonder how they do it and what we are doing wrong that at times makes it so difficult for us to live the writing life.

I wrote *Rut-Busting Book for Writers* because I wanted to figure out how to better live this life I have chosen for myself. My hope is that you too will find it useful and encouraging.

I'd love to hear from you—what you gained from reading *Rut-Busting Book for Writers* as well as what new strategies you have developed to reach your writing goals.

Reach out to me via email at nancy@nancychristie.com or join my *Rut-Busting Book for Writers* Street Team for the latest news, updates and dates for my "Rut-Busting" workshops—just send me an email requesting to be added to the mailing list!

And of course, consider posting a review for *Rut-Busting Book for Writers*. Visit my book's webpage (www.rutbustingbookforwriters.com/) for links to your favorite retailer.

Thanks so much and happy writing!

Nancy Christie

2017

ACKNOWLEDGMENTS

So many people have helpd to bring this book to fruition, and they deserve both credit and my gratitude.

Ann Henry, my eagle-eyed editor, who not only edited the manuscript and suggested improvements but also encouraged me when I was filled with self-doubt.

My Monday Night Writers group, who gave me feedback on the chapters and ideas for topics to cover. A special shout-out to members Anita Gorman and Cliff Protzman who also contributed their insights to the book.

All those I have interviewed on my blogs (One on One: Insights Into the Writer's Life, The Writer's Place and Focus on Fiction), for sharing their experiences as writers that ultimately formed the basis for this book.

My contributors, who provided their insights, wisdom and suggestions about living the writing life.

And all the writers I have met along the way—at my workshops, at conferences, and other writing events—who inspired me to write this book.

INTRODUCTION

"Writing is like daydreaming with a purpose."
Wendy Janes

I write because I love to write. Writing gives me the best and perhaps the only way to express what I am thinking and feeling, what I have come to understand and what I have yet to unravel. I write because it is as natural to me as breathing—*and* as essential.

And I write because it's the one thing I know I can do, make a living at and take great pride in—and for all the other reasons that author Wendy Janes listed: "to share my stories, to entertain, to encourage people to think, perhaps to teach them, and on occasion to comfort. Writing gives me the opportunity to make a connection with people, many of whom I wouldn't be able to connect with otherwise."

But the fact that it is my choice doesn't mean that it's been an entirely easy path to follow. There have been more than a few challenges along the way: stories, articles and manuscripts that were rejected, clients who paid too little, and days, weeks and sometimes years when I didn't write, *couldn't* write and despaired of ever being able to write again.

And while sometimes the setbacks were due to events outside my control, more than a few times the cause can be traced back to something I did or didn't do, choices I made that either landed me squarely in a writing rut or made the one I was in even deeper.

THE POWER OF PASSION

"Writing for me is like a bridge between myself and the rest of the universe." Tim Quigley

By its very nature, writing is a solitary pursuit. Even if you belong to a writing group or take writing classes, spend your writing time in a café or library, the reality is that, wherever you are and whomever you are surrounded by, you are still alone in your head, writing.

And that very aloneness can lead to a host of conflicting emotions about yourself and your writing ability. You love to write and can't imagine doing anything else, but then... you learn that a writer friend got an agent and you wonder what's wrong with you that you don't have one.

Another writer had his article accepted and you ask yourself why all you receive are rejections. Or after attending a workshop on freelance writing where everyone else talks about their six-figure incomes, you look at your last year's profit-and-loss statement and see that it reflects just a five-figure one—in the *low* five figures, no less.

When the writing isn't going well—or isn't going at all!—it's so easy to wonder *why* you are doing it, if you're being foolish or selfish to devote time to what could be considered a long shot instead of making a more practical and reasonable choice. And along the way, you lose sight of the motivation that drives you to put pen to paper or fingers to keyboard.

The reality is that it's not always so easy to feel good about writing—or about yourself as a writer. Your expectations about what being a writer should be (triggered by the comparison game) can often make you doubt yourself and your abilities.

You imagine that all the other writers wake up each morning full of confidence and creative fire and go to bed each night satisfied with their literary accomplishments. And because you don't always feel that way, you put yourself in a different class or on a lower level—or maybe not even in the "writer" category at all.

When I hold my "Rut-Busting" Workshops for Writers, one of the very first activities I have the participants do is introduce themselves to all the other attendees. But this is no quick "Hi, I'm Mary" exercise. Instead, each one has to follow the same script: "Hi, I'm Mary, and I'm a successful writer," or "Hi, I'm Joe, and I'm a successful writer."

While there's always a certain amount of laughter during the exercise, it's obvious that some people have trouble using the word "successful" while others balk at claiming the title "writer." Their responses go something like this:

- "I'm not really a writer. I mean, I write **but** I haven't been published."

- "Successful? Not really. I'm working on something **but** I don't know if I can finish it."

- "I've had a story [or a poem or an essay] published **but** I didn't get paid, so I guess I'm not a real writer."

All those "buts" that need to be busted!

The only requirement to claim the title of "successful writer" is that you write as *often* as you can, as *much* as you can and to the best of your ability. Isaac Asimov said it best in *Gold* when he defined writers as those who consistently work at their craft, even if they are unknown to the world or never earn any publishing credits or income from their work.

You can't look to external sources for your validation as a writer because that puts you at the mercy of readers and reviewers, people who measure your ability by the money you've been paid or the places you've been published. Then, when the responses are not what you hoped for—or fail to materialize at all—your confidence in your ability begins to drain away and your passion for writing starts to fade.

Instead, you must feed the flame through the work itself— from the way it makes you feel to express your thoughts and emotions in a fixed fashion.

Author Julie Anne Lindsey first experienced this when she was writing her debut novel. "I realized I'd found my passion and calling in a place I'd never expected. I felt it instinctively. I was meant to do this. I just had to figure out how," she said, adding, "I get incredible joy and satisfaction from the writing process. I love being an author. I love the daily challenge, the research, the creation, all of it. I love the readers, fellow authors and the industry at large. This is right where I belong."

A key point in Lindsey's response is that her sense of fulfillment isn't grounded in book sales or royalty checks but in how the writing process makes her feel. And it's that positive, self-affirming emotion that keeps her pursuing her craft.

Remember: You are a writer as long as you write. How you identify yourself with regard to your writing can make all the difference. It can either ignite your passion or dampen it to the point where the flame flickers and finally dies out.

The second rule is to think about your reasons for writing. *Why* do you want to write? What does the act of writing *bring* into your life? I've asked those two questions of the many writers that I've interviewed over the years, and the answers vary as much as the type of writing they do.

For Catherine Wald, working on her book, *The Resilient Writer: Tales of Rejection and Triumph by 23 Top Authors*, led to some realizations about her reasons for writing.

"I wrote *The Resilient Writer* because I was overwhelmed with frustration when my agented novel was rejected by a dozen or more publishers. One thing I learned about myself personally—and I think others share this—is that I had a Cinderella-like fantasy about being a published and of course successful writer. Fame was a stand-in for Prince Charming, who would fill my life with excitement and romance. I expected not only success but a life-changing experience."

But then Wald did some serious soul-searching about her definition of success. "I wanted to live a life connected to people who cared about writing and the arts," she explained. "I wanted to continue to write what I wanted and to grow as a writer, an artist, and a citizen of the writing community. And I realized that I didn't actually have to become famous to do that. It would have helped, but there is so much one can do without needing a stamp of approval from anyone."

Writing can also be a way of processing life events as in the case of author and freelance writer Maria Ciletti. She used journal writing to document her experiences during the four years she cared for her mother, who had been diagnosed with Alzheimer's disease.

"I wrote what I was feeling, what she was feeling, and all the challenges we faced during that difficult time," she said, with her journal forming the basis of her book, *I Have to Leave You Now: A Survival Guide for Caregivers of Loved Ones with Alzheimer's Disease.*

Short-story writer Tim Quigley is driven by "a need to share what I see, what I think, and what I feel. If I don't do it, then I have this other sense of incompletion and frustration that follows me around as well, like this cosmic and perpetual to-do list."

Author and world traveler Allan Karl said that he can't help "creating stories in my mind of people I observe as I travel. I have an incredible passion to understand and learn the stories, background and motivations of most anyone I meet or who catches my mind."

Karl views writing as a way to be open to new ideas, to change, to different food, people and culture that ultimately leads to understanding and learning, a similar concept expressed by crime fiction writer Marie Sutro.

"Creating credible characters requires empathy," she noted. "Without opening your mind to other people's circumstances and the factors that motivate or impede them, it is almost impossible to create an authentic human experience for the reader."

For author Jessica Soffer, writing "brings as much to my life (joy, understanding, challenge, ritual) as it is my life. Writing is the way that I process and communicate and organize my thoughts and my time."

While noting that "none of my work is autobiographical," romance writer Jamie Beck said, "I need to write because the stories want to be told. I suppose it is cathartic, too. I'm sure I'm working out 'new' endings to some of my own old wounds in these books."

So many writers said that writing isn't just something they *choose* to do, but also something they *have* to do—a creative expression that fulfills them like nothing else. As young-adult author Heidi Angell said, "Even if I could never have my work read by others, I don't think I would stop writing."

Author Gillian Felix said, "Writing takes me into a world that I would never have the chance to be a part of. It is my escape. I love the whole creative process, the research and the thoughts and emotions that come from it. It is very therapeutic for me," adding perhaps only partly tongue-in-cheek, "Why do I want to write? What else is there for me to do?"

It's the process, even more so than the result—fame, fortune, publication—that drives so many writers. Not that being recognized as a writer or having an SRO crowd for a book signing isn't a thrill! But eventually, it all comes down to just you and the blank sheet or screen, and without feeling the passion for writing alive in you, you can find it well-nigh impossible to start again.

So how do you know if you have that passion? How can you identify those times when the desire to write has burned most strongly inside you? Ask yourself:

- Have you ever become so involved in a writing project that you forget where you are or how you feel, forget about what is worrying or upsetting you?

- Have you ever felt so committed to writing that nothing else matters—not how hard you have to work at it or how much time you are spending doing it?

- When you are engaged in writing, does it make you feel better about yourself? Do you feel like this is what you were meant to be doing, that you are using the gift—the talent and ability—that you were given?

If you answered "yes" to any of these questions, then you have found your writing passion. Passion takes you out of yourself and beyond your own needs and awareness. It transports you to a place where time and effort are meaningless. When you spend time doing that about which you feel most passionate, you fill your life with energy and joy.

That being said, don't expect to feel that same white-hot fire every time you sit down to write. Sometimes, the sensation is just simple pleasure. You are enjoying what you are doing but are not necessarily overwhelmed with emotion.

Other times, what you are writing can generate a far deeper, more intense response: you laugh or cry, your pulse quickens, you end your writing session as exhausted as if you had just run a marathon.

I have experienced this range of responses in my own writing life. As a full-time freelance copywriter, I write for a living, and while my work doesn't produce the same high level of emotional involvement as writing fiction or essays, I still enjoy what I am doing. I challenge myself, trying to achieve my self-set level of perfection—if achieving perfection is *ever* possible!

And I can be as pleased with the outcome of a marketing piece as I can be with that of a short story because both caused me to tap into my creativity in new and different ways.

You need to view your relationship with your writing as a love affair. There are times when you can't wait to be with your "writing lover," when you lose yourself in the tactile nature of the craft— the sensation of the pen in your hand, the touch of the keyboard to your fingertips—or when the urge to express yourself is like a siren's song pulling you toward writing.

And then there are the times when writing is less passionate but more comfortable, giving you a sense of security and belonging, of being where you should be doing what you ought to do. Both conditions should be equally appreciated.

Finally, think about the concept of success: what being successful means to you, how you define it, how you will know that you have achieved it. In his blog post, "How to sell loads of books," author Russell Blake noted that while writing "is art and self-expression, something beautiful and intensely personal," selling books or, for that matter, any sales resulting from what you have written, "is a commercial enterprise. Confuse the two, and you hurt any chances you have of success, if success to you means selling a bunch of books."

Only you know how you define success, but using the marketplace's valuation—the number of books sold or pieces accepted— can make it difficult for you to keep going. The fact is, there will always be someone else who will sell more books than you will, make more money than you do, be better known than you are. There may be pieces that you write that bring you a great deal of joy and satisfaction because you have stretched your writing gift in a new way or explored a subject that you had hitherto avoided, yet they will never be read by anyone other than you.

There's nothing wrong with wanting to achieve a level of fame and fortune through your writing. I'll be the first to admit that I regularly check sales figures for my books and lustily blow my own horn when an essay or short story has been accepted for publication or when I receive a great review for one of my books. But that's not the reason why I write, only a very happy by-product.

If I started each piece by asking myself, "Will someone want to read this? Publish this?", then a lot of the writing I do wouldn't have seen the light of day. I write first to understand what I am thinking and feeling, what I have witnessed and what I imagine I have seen. Many of my essays and short stories are yet to be published, but that doesn't make them any less worth the time I gave them.

Some stories, like "Annabelle," didn't reach the reading public until decades after I wrote them. I wrote the first draft of "Annabelle" in 1989, refined it off and on over a period of years, and then submitted it to numerous publications before it was finally published in my first collection, *Traveling Left of Center and Other Stories*.

And I freely admit that the praise it received was gratifying— and yes, I *so* wanted to send an email to all those editors who had rejected it! I didn't, of course, because fiction is very subjective: what is pleasing to one editor's palate can be bland to another's.

But the point is that just because your work is rejected doesn't mean you *can't* write. It could mean that you have to cultivate your ability or improve your skills—something, in fact, that *all* writers should be doing as a matter of course. It could also mean that you sent it to the wrong market or the subject matter is one that doesn't currently appeal to readers.

Whether you do it for money or simply for love, whether everyone reads your work or no one has even heard of you, the act of writing, in and of itself, is something to be honored. It brings you a sense of completeness and joy, the realization that you are doing not only what you want to do but also what you are meant to do.

And understanding that, you know that you must continue to write, no matter what. You must stoke the fire of creativity with whatever fuel works for you and only stop when you have run out of things to say, topics to explore, emotions to uncover, stories to tell. And as long as your passion for writing is burning, that will never happen.

WHAT'S YOUR RUT?

"If you're not scared, you're not writing...A state of anxiety is the writer's natural habitat."
Ralph Keyes (from The Courage to Write)

You are passionate about your writing and that's the way it should be. But while feeling passion for your craft is an integral part of the writing life, you can't ignore those impediments that periodically get in your way—those writing ruts you fall into and have to crawl out of—if you're going to pursue a writing career to any level.

And those types of writing ruts can vary, depending on what's happening in your life in general and your creative life in particular.

Let's look at three of the more common ones.

- The Comfort Rut—Settling for where you are in your writing life rather than stretching your creative abilities: the "This is what I do best so that's what I'm sticking with!" excuse.

- The Fear Rut—Holding back from trying something new, whether it's writing in a different genre, promoting yourself and your work, or committing to writing in general: the "What if I fail? I'll make a fool of myself!" defense.

- The Negativity Rut—Believing that the odds are against your ever achieving anything with your writing: the "No one will want to hire me/publish me/read my work so why bother?" rationale.

The Comfort Rut

A comfort rut is the tendency to stay within the same type of writing that you've been doing to avoid challenging yourself. Why is it called a "comfort rut"? Because it's *comfortable*.

Let's face it, exploring a new type of writing can be a little scary since it brings up the prospect of failure. Far easier to stay with what you do and do well, writing what is accepted by friends, editors and publishers and your reading public. You've established yourself, you know the space you're in and you can churn out words relatively easily. Why venture into the unknown?

While the comfort rut might feel safe and secure to you, it is doing *nothing* to help you explore all your creative potential.

- Just because you've been writing nonfiction doesn't mean that somewhere inside your writing brain there might not be an imaginary character and plot trying to get out. As Sally Koslow, former editor, essayist and article writer, detailed on her website, she had that experience after her job as the first editor-in-chief of *Lifetime* magazine ended. She then joined a writing group to explore fiction writing and ultimately wrote her first novel, *Little Pink Slips*.

- Just because you've established a following writing spy stories doesn't mean juvenile literature is outside the realm of possibilities. Ian Fleming of James Bond fame pulled it off with *Chitty Chitty Bang Bang*, wrote author and writing expert Joanna Penn in her "Can authors be successful in multiple genres?" post.

- Just because you write romance novels doesn't mean you can't write detective stories. Nora Roberts did it and wrote her crime stories under the name of J.D. Robb, pointed out Summerita Rhayne in her post, "The Pros and Cons of Switching Genres," on Jami Gold's blog.

Or, for that matter, just because you make your living writing marketing copy for hospitals or governmental entities doesn't mean you can't shift into other types of writing, such as video scripts or case studies, or write for other industries, such as manufacturers or retailers.

"But I'm doing okay with what I'm writing!" you protest. "*I* like it! Why should I change?"

A couple of reasons. Let's start with simple economics, and I'll use my own experience as an example. For years, the bulk of my time and the primary source of my income was related to writing magazine articles for trade and consumer publications. The money was good, I was paid regularly and I liked the work. Granted, it wasn't as creatively fulfilling as writing fiction, but it paid the bills and kept a roof over my head.

Then came the recession of 2007, and magazines began closing their doors to freelancers or, in some cases, closing their doors entirely. Not good news for anybody, including me since writing was my sole source of income.

While I had also been doing a small amount of corporate writing, I had to improve my content writing *and* marketing skills if I was going to continue as a freelancer. That experience taught me a valuable lesson: to survive as a writer, you not only have to continue to improve your current skill level but also expand into new areas so you're ready for market changes.

"But," you say, "this doesn't apply to me. I write *books!*"

Remember, readers' tastes change as well, and what was popular last year or three years ago may not be the go-to choice today or next year. Granted, your fan base may continue to read your books, but you should always be increasing your readership. For some writers, this may mean branching out into other genres or types of writing, perhaps using a pseudonym so as not to confuse people who see your name, expect a romance and find, instead, a crime novel.

Current real-life events can also inspire you to change what you want to explore in your writing. For example, as climate change becomes more and more of a "hot topic" (no pun intended), it has entered into the literary marketplace with fiction authors exploring the reality and consequences of environmental issues, a trend Michael Berry noted in his Salon.com article, "The rise of climate fiction: When literature takes on global warming and devastating droughts."

Cli-fi (an abbreviation for the climate fiction genre) has been embraced by a number of authors including Michael Crichton, Gareth Renowden, Barbara Kingsolver, Nathaniel Rich and Margaret Atwood. Does this mean you should jump onto the cli-fi bandwagon? Not if it doesn't appeal to you as a topic you want to write about. But if you have an interest in the subject and want to explore it within a fiction construct, then by all means go for it, even if your work to date has been focused on bodice-rippers, not weather changes.

Finally, even if the market and the readership remain consistent, *you* are changing. You may discover that events in your personal life influence your choice of writing, whether in topic or in form. You find and lose people, you experience career or personal crises, you move, literally or metaphorically. Or you may simply have grown tired of one type of writing and want to try something else.

Whatever the reason, you begin to think about expanding into other genres but then start questioning your judgment or ability. Writing is hard enough, you think. Why make it even more challenging by exploring new terrain, creatively speaking?

Why? Because that is how you improve your writing ability. Writing poetry can increase your awareness of rhythm while writing about nature can sharpen your attentiveness to detail—both easily transferable skills to other types of writing. Even if you only switch genre gears for yourself, not for publication, it has a useful purpose since it opens your creative mind to new ways of expressing thoughts, emotions and realizations.

In her post, "Can authors be successful in multiple genres?" on her The Creative Penn blog, Penn wrote about that challenge when she wanted to move beyond nonfiction to explore other genres. She took the leap into fiction, writing two novel series—action adventure thrillers and crime thrillers—as well as several fantasy novels and short stories, all under the name of J.F. Penn, making her a best-selling author in both fiction and nonfiction!

She chose to use a pseudonym and created two separate websites to differentiate between her two "brands" because, as she explained, "the target market for TheCreativePenn.com and my nonfiction books is very different from the people who want to read my fiction and check out JFPenn.com. I needed to keep the two audiences separate."

Writer and editor Paige Duke provided an interesting take on the topic of pseudonyms in her article, "Should You Write Under A Pen Name?" on the Standout Books website. Duke listed three reasons for choosing a pen name: having a name that is the same name as someone who is famous, is too hard to spell, or isn't a good fit for your genre.

You might also consider it if you need a fresh start, she said. "Sometimes you just need to start over. If authors' early novels don't sell well, they may have trouble getting a second chance under their own name. Taking a pen name is a great solution to that problem."

But, she added, "if the genres aren't too dissimilar, it might actually work in your favor to keep writing under your name in order to retain your readership."

The goal is to do something different, not more of the same, to generate a sense of excitement around the writing process. And sometimes, when you make that change, it can also alter how you look at life—both in and outside of your writing existence.

The Fear Rut

Sometimes the resistance is fear-based. You are afraid of making the change because you have to "go into the dark"—enter an unfamiliar place, creatively speaking. And the dark can be a very scary place. You not only don't know what to expect, you are afraid that you can't handle the challenge—that you just don't have it in you.

It's all about a little four-letter word that can be a really big problem: FEAR. Just the thought of trying something new gives a weird and not at all pleasant feeling that you believe is some kind of warning that you can't do it, that you are going to fail, or that, in that unknown territory, there be dragons, a cautionary notation medieval mapmakers used on uncharted areas.

But fear is just a *feeling*—it's not a prediction of how things are going to turn out, something I learned back in 2000. A friend of mine, Kelly Boyer Sagert, was the host of a local cable show, and she had invited me to be on her program to talk about writing.

But I resisted most strongly. Not that I couldn't *talk* about writing—I taught classes on it all the time! But this was on television! I never *did* TV before. And somehow, being on the small screen was far more frightening than standing up in front of a group of writing students!

So, I did what any coward would do—I said, "No. No way. Ain't happening."

And when she asked me why I was refusing, I gave her what I thought was a pretty logical reason: "Because I never did it before." Her response? "I try never to confuse 'I haven't done it' with 'I can't do it.'" That pretty much shot down my excuse.

I gave in and, despite my almost paralyzing fear of the camera, took my seat in the guest chair and for about 20 minutes talked about writing. And it actually wasn't as frightening or awful as I had feared! In fact, I loved it! More importantly, I learned a valuable lesson: just because I *haven't* done it before doesn't mean I *can't* do it.

And now every time a new opportunity comes along—whether it's an assignment for a client that's a new challenge for me or the chance to speak before a group—I just say "yes." And when those fear-based phrases start rolling around in my head—*I can't do this. I'll fail. This is too hard/too new/ too challenging*—I shut them down by asking myself what's the worst that can happen?

Even if I fail, it's not a life-ending outcome. And no matter what, whether I do great, do lousy or fall somewhere in between, I'll learn something about myself and my abilities and what to do—or not do—next time!

Interestingly, while Sagert's words have influenced my decision-making process, she had fallen into the same "I can't because I haven't" rut. In 2008, she had the opportunity to submit a play to be produced by Lorain County Metroparks and TrueNorth Cultural Arts.

The only problem, said Sagert, "was that I wrote mostly nonfiction and I certainly didn't do performance kind of things. My friend Rick Fortney, who was managing that community theater group, gave me the information and said I should consider it. But I said, 'I'm not going to enter a playwriting contest. I've never done it before. Absolutely not.'"

What tipped the scales for Sagert was that one of the topics was the Underground Railroad, which was a huge passion of hers. "I changed my mind and told my friend that I'd send him a proposal." The play was eventually produced and, Sagert said, "I absolutely loved the experience! It was one of the highlights of my writing career!"

That play led to a second one as well as other performance-style pieces, and ultimately to her most recent one, a PBS-sponsored documentary called "Trail Magic: The Grandma Gatewood Story" that has been nominated for an Emmy.

"If an opportunity came up to write another play I wouldn't say no," said Sagert, adding, "And now I am taking two playwriting classes! I think I really should know how to do this now that people think I can!"

Taking a chance on yourself is the only way you will get out of your fear rut. But that approach comes with a word of advice: don't get bogged down in the quest for perfection. This is a learning exercise, and like all learning exercises, there is a built-in sequence of trying, failing and trying again.

Think about what happens when a baby learns to walk. The first time he falls down, the parents don't rush over and say, "Oh, no, how could you be so stupid? You had better not do that again because you could get hurt!" No, they praise him for the attempt and encourage him to try it again.

That's what you need to do for yourself: give it—whatever "it" is—a try. Will the experience always turn out the way you want, even when you give it your best shot? Of course not. But I can guarantee that if you don't push past the fear and go for it, you will never know. And if it doesn't work out as well as you hoped, try again. It's all about making the effort, not necessarily achieving success.

To reinforce that, take a little stroll down memory lane. Review some of the writing from your early days when you were just starting out. This little exercise should highlight how far you have come and how many ways you have improved your writing skills.

Also, expect that your faith in yourself and your writing ability will hit highs and lows, so don't be surprised if some days you feel that you are just one article away from a Pulitzer while other days you think your work isn't even good enough to line a bird cage!

Writer Barbara Routen said, "My writing confidence meanders between 'I am invincible' and 'I can't do this,' hitting all points along the way. My goal always is to do my best, so I work hard, seek pointers from other writers individually and in writing groups, read great literature, study works in other publications and genres, attend conferences and consult writing blogs. Online dictionaries, thesauruses and grammar sites are my best friends."

While she noted that most of the time she is "healthily confident," she added, "Sometimes, I get in a slump and have to force myself to write. I then must submit the result, no matter what I've created, to meet my deadline. I may or may not have produced my finest, most-compelling work but I accept that I've done the best I can under the circumstances. It helps to know my editors may question, make suggestions and help me improve my work as needed. I trust that eventually I'll be in my self-assured frame of mind again."

While all writers, as young adult-fantasy novelist Lorraine Ambers pointed out, probably suffer from crippling self-doubt from time to time, the challenge is to keep it from stopping you.

"I have suffered from stress and anxiety. When that happens, my creativity shuts down. I'm on standstill, stuck in a world of procrastination where the beast of fear attacks in full force," she said, adding, "I have purposely pushed through the fear, by taking small steps and setting little daily goals that are achievable. I do this knowing what the end goal is and by having faith in my abilities."

The Negativity Rut

- *"Nobody ever gets published unless they know somebody in the business."*

- *"The magazine industry is almost impossible to break into."*

- *"I can't write like all those other writers. I'm just no good."*

Hmmm…Heard those words before? Have you *spoken* some variation of them to others or to yourself? Is that *really* what you believe when you think of being a writer? Does the word "negativity" spring to mind?

You might think you're being objective or realistic, but the truth is you are feeding yourself a big helping of hopelessness seasoned with a heavy dose of pessimism. And with *that* on the menu, you're liable to be stuck in your negativity rut for a good long while.

If you find that you are feeling negative way too often, pay attention to the words you are using and the thoughts you are having about writing. Writers know how powerful words are, but we so rarely listen to what we are saying and thinking! Where our attention goes, energy flows, and our thoughts and words direct our attention.

If you focus on failure or talk about how hard the industry is, then you *will* fail and the industry *will* be a hard one indeed. Each time you think or say something negative about the industry or your own ability, stop and counter it with a positive statement.

Predicting failure is a surefire way to guarantee failure. Better to spend your time and energy focusing on positive outcomes and doing everything you can to make them come true. Instead of saying, "I'll send this pitch out, but I'm sure it will be rejected," try "I'll send this pitch out, and if it comes back, I'll find a new market." Instead of saying, "Agents and publishers won't want to see my work," try "I'll research what they are looking for until I find some that are a good match for my project."

What if you're not sure if you're in a writing rut? Well, if you're doing the same kind of writing that you were doing last year, if you have consistently avoided stretching yourself artistically, if you are far better at creating excuses than creating new pieces, then you are probably in a rut!

The reality is that throughout your writing life you may fall into different ruts. But while it's normal to get trapped in one, it doesn't mean that you should accept it as your personal status quo. Instead, view the situation as a challenge, see it as a need to shake things up, and regard it as an opportunity to take on your preconceptions about the writing life and prove them wrong.

In short, *write* your way out of your writing rut!

YOUR WRITING "ROAD MAP"

"A temporary delay does not mean a permanent detour from your writing goals. Pick up that pen and begin again." Sharon C. Jenkins

Figuring out which rut you're in is only *part* of the process. Even if you successfully clambered out of the ditch, you *still* need to know where you are heading and what's the best strategy for getting there. What does this involve? Setting goals and creating a plan to achieve them. Determining your destination and developing an itinerary that will get you there.

And most importantly, stop *talking* about what you're *going* to do and start *doing* it!

When I saw the movie *Joy* starring Jennifer Lawrence as inventor and entrepreneur Joy Mangano, my take on the underlying message was that it wasn't just about *having* a dream, but also *committing* to it and making it a *priority*. Doing what you need to do, no matter what. Even if you have a talent and gift for writing, even if you tell everyone in earshot that you want to write, that you *have* to write, if you don't actually *do* it, then it isn't going to happen. And that's where the Writing Roadmap fits in.

It's a three-part process:

- First, you identify your short- and long-term goals.

- Second, you set a start time and deadline.

- Third, you create an Action Plan for each goal.

Step 1: Define Your Short- and Long-Term Goals

Setting goals is like taking a trip. You need to know your destination before you start on your journey. In this case, you need to know where you want to end up as a writer before you begin your literary expedition. It sounds a little like *Alice in Wonderland*—begin at the end and work backwards—but it actually makes a lot of sense. You have to know your goals before you can develop a strategy for achieving them.

What are your writing goals: to make a name for yourself as a writer, to give your creativity the time and space to come forth, to write for pleasure or money or maybe even both? In my case, when I first started freelancing, writing books wasn't even on my radar. My one and only goal was to make enough money writing for clients and magazines that I could quit my day job.

When that occurred back in 1996, then I added a second goal that spoke to my passion for writing fiction. I wanted to have time to write and submit short stories, so I had to fit that one into my schedule.

Now, more than twenty years and several books and published short stories later, my long-term goal of building a reputation as a fiction and nonfiction author and short story writer takes up a higher proportion of my time.

Short-term? Finish individual book projects, actively seek literary representation and gain more speaking engagements. Of course, to be able to do all those, I still need to have an income, so my second goal is to continue to build my client base so there are always assignments coming in, which also involves expanding my own skill set so I have more to offer.

As this illustrates, goal setting is an ongoing and fluid process. As you achieve one goal, you revise your overall plan. Or if, for whatever reason, one of your goals is no longer an option, you either "back-burner" it (put it to one side and not spend time actively pursuing it) or jettison it entirely.

What are your long-range plans for your writing career? Where do you want to be at the end of the next twelve months, in five years, in ten? Now narrow your focus: what do you have to do this month, this week, today to make it happen? What single task executed to the best of your ability will move your marker farther down the line?

Write it down—write it *all* down. As a writer, you know how powerful words can be, especially when they are committed to paper.

"Having your goals clearly written down …will help you to stay determined and focused…[and] concentrate your mind on one desired outcome (and the steps needed to see it to completion)," wrote motivational speaker Sooraj Singh in "The Top 7 Benefits of Writing Down Your Goals" post on the Get Motivation blog. "Without knowing what to do, you can do nothing."

So make your list then hang it somewhere highly visible. That way, every day you are reminded of what you have committed to doing. Creating a goals list is essential because if you don't know *what* your writing goals are, you won't be able to achieve them!

Add in Specific Details

Sounds pretty simple, doesn't it? Just write down what you want. But now it's time for some editing to look for those goals that are more generalizations than specific and definable aims.

For example, suppose you listed "write more" as your number one goal. Okay. How much more? Ten minutes a day? Ten hours a week? Ten thousand words a month? Maybe your goal is to pitch more articles. Sounds good, but let's improve it. Add in a quantifiable measure: "Have 15 magazine queries circulating at any given time."

Or perhaps your goal is to make a living as a writer—go the freelance route. This also requires a few more details. Will you be writing for magazines or corporate clients? And what is your definition of "making a living"? Earning $10,000 a year? $100,000 a year? Numbers factor into goal setting as anyone who has tried to lose weight knows! It's all about the numbers on the scale.

Asking yourself these questions as you review each item on your goal list will help you figure out exactly what you want and track your progress so you know when you are close to achieving it.

Along with parameters, you need to make sure the goals you choose are ones over which you have control. I can't set a goal of "secure literary representation" since I don't control decisions made at literary agencies. But I *can* control "actively seek literary representation" because I am responsible for researching agencies where I can submit my book proposals and manuscripts.

In his Training Peaks' post, "10 Guidelines for Effective Goal Setting," USA Triathlon-certified coach and American College of Sports Medicine-certified personal trainer Adam Hodges wrote about the need to focus more on performance- and process-related goals versus outcome-related goals.

"While outcome goals provide long-term motivation and many long-term goals take this form," he explained, "performance and process goals help us focus on what we need to do in the intermediate and short-term, such as in the moment of the race."

This is true whether you are running a marathon or working on a book—a marathon of its own, so to speak.

Evaluate Your Reasons for Choosing Those Goals

The next part of goal setting deals with the "why" factor: the reason behind that particular goal. Why is knowing that important? Because if you have the wrong reason for working toward it, your chances of *achieving* success or being satisfied with it if it *does* occur are greatly reduced.

For example, you want to be a freelance writer. Okay, good goal. But if your reason for that goal is that you think it will be easier than working for someone else, you are in for a rude awakening.

There is nothing easy about being self-employed as those who have run their own businesses will tell you. There's no one to pass the buck to, as the saying goes, since you are the one in charge. Both the bucks (i.e., complaints and problems) *and* the bills land on your desk. So if your motivation is because you're tired of being told *what* to do, *how* to do it and *when* to have it completed, you won't be able to handle being both the person giving the orders and the person responsible for carrying them out.

Maybe your goal is to write the Great American Novel so you can become rich and famous—right away! You envision sitting back in your comfortable easy chair in your well-appointed writing space and opening royalty checks one after another, or appearing at bookstores where the line of fans stretches down the aisle and out the door and the media people crowd around you anxiously awaiting their turn to do an interview.

You don't see the flaw in your expectations and are completely unprepared for the work involved and the setbacks you'll encounter: the rejected submissions, the hours spent writing, then rewriting, then revising yet again, and (assuming your book gets published) the book signing events where the only question store patrons ask is "Where's the restroom?"

The writing goal you have set has to be the right one for you and based on reality, not fantasy. Understanding *why* you want to achieve something is just as important as knowing *what* it is you want to achieve. No matter how laudable a goal may be, if your motivations are wrong, you will find it difficult if not impossible to be successful.

And if you do succeed, chances are you won't be happy with the outcome.

Step 2: Set Your Start Time and Deadline

Start times, deadlines and all the little time stages in between…setting those can be a challenge for all you procrastinators out there.

Once you've analyzed your goal and decided it's the right one, you need to set start times and deadlines. These are critical for achieving your goal since they serve two purposes: they keep you from adopting a "someday" attitude and also create a framework to include the steps you need to take to move from the ground floor to the attic, so to speak.

For example, New Year's Day is traditionally a time when we make our list of writing goals. And the list usually starts out with "This year I will…" But they often don't have an actual calendar date associated with them. What you need for success is a clearly defined "start time" as opposed to the more amorphous "when I have some time." You must pick a specific date and set it in stone, then follow through—no matter what.

Deadlines… Along with your start time is your deadline, a concept you're undoubtedly familiar with if you write for publication. But when it comes to setting personal writing goals—finishing the novel or starting a freelance business—you may find that you tend to make the deadlines very open-ended, along the lines of "someday before I die…"

Or, if you do set them, you leave yourself lots of wiggle room using words like "hopefully" and "plan to" and "as long as" instead of the more definite and committed "will" as in: "By March 1, I will have the first draft finished." The tendency to keep deadlines open or less than definite explains why so many New Year's resolutions are recycled, year after year!

When you set your writing goals, establish deadlines for achieving them. If it's an ongoing goal—for example, pitching so many articles in a given time period—set a date for evaluating your progress.

If it's a goal that will take months or even years to accomplish, like writing a book, set mini-deadlines for when each chapter will be completed along with your final deadline when the book will be done. Those mini-deadlines are your benchmarks—times when you stop, review how far you have come, evaluate how far you have left to go, and determine if you are still on track or if, somewhere along the way, you have drifted off course.

Also, it's not enough to know when you're going to start it or when you want to reach the end. You need to have a realistic idea of how long the goal will take—not an idealized concept. You probably *can't* write a book from scratch in 30 days—or at least, not and have it ready for publication. Everything takes time.

Establish a reasonable expectation of the length of time it's going to take and then review your progress at regular intervals to adjust the schedule for those delays that inevitably occur.

When you're setting your time frames, you also need to look at one other kind of "time": life-time. Is this the right time in your life to go after this particular goal? Are you in the right place, financially or emotionally, to work on this project?

Your goal needs to fit with where you are right now in your life and in relation to your other obligations. You may *want* to freelance full time, may even *have* all the skills and attributes necessary to achieve it, but your family obligations may not afford you the time to do it or the financial support to take the risk.

Sometimes the goal needs to be delayed or modified because of life circumstances that either *can't* be changed or carry equal or even *more* weight.

Step 3: Create an Action Plan

Your Action Plan is your task list: what you need to do to move from Point A to Point B—or Z. It gives you a structure to work within and allows you to make adjustments as circumstances change. An Action Plan also comes into play as you evaluate your own potential for achieving your goal or when you need to add additional steps to ensure your success.

Do you have the talent and education it will require? Are you ready now, or do you need more training and experience? For example, going back to the freelancing goal, if you expect the money to roll right in despite your not having a strong business background, knowledge of the clientele you plan on approaching and limited writing experience, it's probably not an attainable goal at this moment.

You may find that you need to insert more steps into your Action Plan or adjust your overall timetable based on the individual stages you have to complete.

At this point, you may be feeling a bit overwhelmed by the whole goal-setting process—understandable, especially if you are new to formulating life plans. So start small: take one of your goals and set your start time and deadline.

Then list the broad categories related to that goal that must be completed. Using full-time freelancing as an example, this might include identifying your marketable skills, determining your target market, understanding the business requirements of the profession and learning how to market your services.

Take each category and break it down into tasks: those activities you need to do or steps you need to take to satisfy the requirements of that category, setting individual start times and deadlines for each. These are your mini-deadlines and serve as a way to evaluate how well you are working toward your ultimate goal.

Finally, working backward from your deadline, determine what you need to do each day, week or month to meet that deadline. Now all you need to do is complete one task by one date. And when you look at it that way, it's more manageable.

This is a useful strategy for making any kind of change since it keeps you focused on the path ahead. It also helps avoid that feeling of "this is so huge an undertaking that I can't possibly do it!" feeling.

RAISING THE BAR

"When writing, write as a craftsman/artist, and strive to improve every day. Force yourself to constantly up your game." Russell Blake

Complacency is a dangerous disease that may infect any writer from time to time. For example, suppose you've had a fair degree of success with the type of writing you've been doing for magazines or clients.

Consequently, you start feeling, well, a little smug. A little too self-assured. A little too "I am very good at what I do and don't have to worry about improving."

And then it happens:

- An editor for a new-to-you publication rejects your latest article with the terse observation that "this is not up to our standards."

- A new client redlines your copy and says that you completely misunderstood the aim of the piece *and* the voice of the company.

- Your creative writing submissions bounce back faster and faster with comments like "there's nothing fresh here" or "it lacks continuity" or, even worse, with no comment at all.

What does this mean? You haven't been challenging yourself, improving your skills or developing better techniques. In short, you haven't been raising the bar.

While a certain level of confidence is necessary to keep the creative fires from going out, too high a level can definitely be too much of a good thing. Writing is a living skill. Each time you pick up a pen or touch the keyboard, some part of you must and should be thinking: Is there a better way to phrase this? Have I explored all the ways I can delineate the character? How else can I open the piece? Is my closing paragraph as strong as it could and should be?

The trick is not to throw out the baby with the bathwater (yes, I know it's a cliché!), meaning don't take away what makes your writing uniquely yours, but instead look for weak areas where you need to step up your game.

So how do you do this?

Learn From Successful Writers

In his book *On Writing – A Memoir of the Craft*, Stephen King advised that writers should both read a lot and write a lot, and it's the first part of that statement I want to focus on. The more you read, whether in your genre or across the writing categories, the more you learn about what works and what doesn't.

For example, you've probably started reading a book or two that you then discarded after the first few pages. Go back to those books and read the sections again, this time with a critical writer's eye. Where did the author lose you? Was it the character development or the lack of a believable plotline? Could you envision the setting or was it just a generic image: a nondescript small town that could be anywhere in the country? Maybe the flaw was in the dialogue—all the characters sounded the same and you had to keep checking who was actually speaking.

Try rewriting a part of the text that had issues and focus on remedying the problems that you encountered. Finally, look at your work. Are you guilty of similar writing sins?

You can also gain an education by reading what works, especially if you choose authors whose skills are in areas where you already know you are challenged. I often find it difficult to fully describe a scene, and it can take many revisions before I have incorporated the key elements that allow a reader to envision what is so clear in my head. And those details matter since painting a "word picture" will help establish the tone of the story and elicit the emotion (fear, excitement, comfort) in your readers you want them to feel.

So to improve my ability, periodically I reread Shirley Jackson's fiction, such as *The Haunting of Hill House,* to examine how she manages to generate the same reaction from me each time I read the stories, even when I know exactly how the piece will end. What physical details did she use to build tension? Why did she choose a time of day or a certain weather condition for that scene? I examine what worked for her and then go back to my own work to see if what I have learned can be applied to specific parts of my story.

Try it with your own writing, comparing a short section with another writer known for excellence in that specific aspect: dialogue, plot, setting or whatever. It's not about copying the style but learning from that writer's use of technique and then incorporating what you've learned into your own work.

Reading the works of other authors is a strategy that writer, theater critic, mosaic artist, and educator Dawn Reno Langley uses since, she said, "I don't think you ever completely learn everything you need to know about being the best writer you can be. Even now, after 30-plus books out, I still seek out techniques that will improve my writing. I read the best writers and the award-winners. If an author has been nominated for a Pulitzer, National Book Award, or Man Booker, I want to read that person's work. Sometimes, I wonder why the book has won an award, but I try to take away something from everything I read, whether it's the rhythm of a sentence or the poetic use of language. I want to learn."

Seek Honest Feedback

Sometimes you claim you want feedback when what you *really* want is approval. But honest feedback is valuable. It tells you what is working and what isn't, where you kept the reader's interest and where the reader is having difficulty following along.

While too many cooks can spoil the broth, as the adage goes, those extra eyes on your project will make all the difference. You might think you have read it carefully and caught all the errors, but as any writer worth his or her salt will tell you, you are not the best proofreader for your own work. You're too close to it and will see what you *think* is there and *miss* the mistakes that are present. Instead, said romance novelist Marie Lavender, after you have "edited your manuscript like crazy, have critique partners and beta readers look over it. If you can afford a professional editor, consider going that route as well."

Where can you find some "extra eyes"? A supportive writer's group is one place, and by "supportive," I mean one in which the members are honest but not harsh. While it can be useful to be part of a group that writes within your genre, you can also learn a lot from those working in other genres. For instance, you may write magazine articles, but even those types of pieces require a certain linguistic rhythm to the words, and a lyricist, trained to identify the cadence and tempo of a piece, can point out areas where your sentences sound "flat."

Or maybe it's in the fiction realm where you lack a certain expertise. You can outline a plot with no problem, but when it comes to describing the nuances of a scene or the hidden elements in the character interactions, your version is almost boringly literal and far too lengthy. A poet, on the other hand, can illustrate emotions and establish relationships with just a few elliptical phrases and will offer suggestions for applying that same technique to your piece.

Writer and author Tara Lynne Groth hosts a writing critique subgroup that is one of many subgroups within Triangle Writers, a group she founded which has more than 900 members. "I meet monthly with my small subgroup and it helps me polish stories before submitting them to journals." For her latest book, *Magazine Queries That Worked: Build Income And Authority With Freelance Journalism*, Groth turned to an editor to help her perfect her manuscript. "He was great to work with and I'm looking forward to using him again for future books."

If you're looking for beta readers, Lavender suggested starting with beta reader discussion groups on Facebook and Google+ to find those who are familiar with your genre. "And don't be afraid to add a few new betas with every manuscript, just to get a different perspective. Who knows? You might find they noticed something no one else did."

I have used beta readers for my books, not only to provide me with technical corrections but also to tell me where the story line may have gotten off-track or where I needed to develop a character more fully. On my go-to beta reader list, I have writers and editors whom I can rely on to identify composition errors—misplaced commas, subject-verb disagreement, plotline problems—as well as readers who are fans of the genre where my current book would fit: women's novels or literary short stories, for example.

The second group may not know if I should have used a semicolon, a colon or an em-dash, but they do know when they are having trouble connecting with my story. They represent my potential market base, and when they tell me what is working and what isn't, I have a chance to fix it before the book is released into the cold, cruel reading world.

If you plan to use beta readers, make your expectations clear from the beginning. What kind of feedback are you looking for: a general comment on whether they liked the piece or a deeper dive into specifics? For example, could they identify with the characters? Was the topic explained well? If you are including artwork, did they find it visually appealing and a good match for the written material?

Also, ask how they will be reading the work: as hard copy, on the computer, or with a smartphone or e-reader? If the piece is going to be released in e-book format, try to find beta readers who use different devices so you can be certain the formatting works and looks good on all of them. For book-length pieces, ask if they have the time to handle the beta-reader process within your timeframe. (You may need to turn in the final draft by a certain date, but if the beta readers aren't aware of your schedule, they make consider it a "when I have a chance" task. After all, they *are* doing it for free!)

As for their comments, while you may not agree with every suggestion a beta or critique partner has for you, Lavender said to be careful in your initial response since "it's easy to let ego get in the way of a good partnership. I like to take the feedback I've received with a grain of salt, while carefully weighing each suggestion. Ask yourself, 'What part of this person's advice can really improve the story here?' Obviously, you should follow your story's vision and honor your characters, but keep an open mind too. That feedback could surprise you. Believe it or not, it may even help you grow as a writer. Imagine that!"

Beta readers can also do more than just review your work and offer suggestions for improvement. For book projects, they can be the start of your "street team," willing to spread the word among their friends, on social networks and with reviews on online bookstores and book sites such as Goodreads and LibraryThing.

Young adult novelist Vicki Leigh created her street team, called Dreamweavers, by first reaching out to her writing and reading friends. "From there, I opened it up to anyone who was interested. My amazing Dreamweavers are the best! They help me spread the news about my books, mostly via social media, and as a thank you for all their help, I regularly do giveaways, and they get sneak peeks on my books and hear news early."

Take a Writing Class

Learning is an ongoing process, and writers devoted to the craft never believe that they know everything about everything related to the profession. Writing classes, whether at educational institutions or at conferences and retreats, can be invaluable for providing you with information and education about all aspects of being a writer.

There are the classes that focus on the craft of writing: fiction, nonfiction, poetry or essay writing. There are sessions that address the business side of writing: pitching, publishing and marketing. You can focus on areas where you know you need help or on one that is completely outside your chosen genre: a class on creative nonfiction even though you write poetry or on article writing although your focus is fiction. Each time you step outside your comfort zone you stretch an unused creative "muscle," and that can translate to an overall gain in your writing ability.

Even though she has an MFA and PhD, Langley said she has "taken more writing courses and workshops than I can possibly count. I will never stop taking workshops, whether online, at a conference, or at a local library."

Groth said she regularly attends conferences, both for writers and for professionals in fields that she specializes in. "For example, one of my journalism and content writing niches is agriculture. I attended a sustainable agriculture conference and selected sessions on food labeling and organic farming practices that helped inspire article ideas, connected me with sources for future articles, and also helped me network with potential clientele," she explained. "When I attend events like that it helps me understand farmers' current challenges, pitch relevant articles, and suggest content based on the state of the industry. I feel it adds more value for readers and clients, and makes me more confident in the work I do."

She also focuses on panels or sessions on topics that she is unfamiliar with to broaden her knowledge base. "One year I attended a crowdfunding panel at the American Society of Journalists and Authors. I knew nothing about crowdfunding. Now, a year or so later, I've launched a crowdfunding campaign for freelancers and used all of my notes from the conference. It's helped me avoid a lot of errors I would have likely made otherwise."

With the availability of online classes and webinars, you aren't limited to in-person classes. Gotham Writers has a list of online courses on its website as well as an extensive resources section. The Master Class website has classes on writing taught by notables that include James Patterson, David Mamet and Shonda Rimes.

You can also check out university-sponsored courses, such as those offered by Massachusetts Institute of Technology's OpenCourseWare, Online Writing Lab (OWL) at Purdue University, Stanford University's Stanford Online and the Writing Center at the University of Iowa. For more formal educational opportunities, check out the writing program tab on *The Writer* website.

Writing magazines' websites are an invaluable source of information. *Writer's Digest* magazine has free webinars while the Poets & Writers Live section on the *Poets & Writers* website features videos, slideshows and audio clips from presentations by noteworthy writers and performers. There are also online classes and informational newsletters available from industry experts who specialize in specific writing-related areas, such as those offered by Jane Friedman and Erika Dreifus.

Classes can also be an effective way to deal with a bad case of "writing boredom"—the approach that author Kelly Boyer Sagert uses. "When I'm bored, I can tell that I'm not challenging myself enough. I start getting that restlessness, which tells me that I've done this—whatever 'this' happens to be—for too long and I've got to do something different. I tend to take a poetry class or a short story class. I go in a different direction just to break out of that rut."

Develop a Self-Study Course

If you are highly motivated and self-disciplined, you could set up a self-study course, using online and print resources to create your personal curriculum.

Start by identifying the area where you know you need improvement. Is it in craft or the business side of writing, i.e., marketing or publishing, for example? Make a list of what you want to know or learn how to do, then start collecting articles and books that deal with that specific topic.

As you work your way through all the resources, take notes (yes, just like in school!), referencing where you found the information. (You'll be glad you did that when you want to go back and check the original source!)

Finally, organize the information in a way that makes it easy for you to follow, either by steps or by sub-categories. For example, I struggle with social media. A *lot*. I either don't know what hashtags to use or, if I do know, I forget to include them. I still write my tweets in full sentences. As for *what* to post *when*, well, my timing is more of the "Rats! I forgot to post that so I better do it now!" variety rather than a well-thought-out schedule.

So I have been gathering articles from newsletters, writing magazines and other resources, sorting them into the categories of social media that I currently use (LinkedIn, Facebook, Twitter and Pinterest) and then listing all the tips and strategies that the experts recommend. It's a long, slow process, but little by little I am getting better!

I also keep all my writing-related books next to my desk and periodically dip into specific ones related to what I may be working on. As I get ready to launch another book, I go back to all those books covering marketing strategies to see what I can do this time around. If I'm back on the literary agent hunt, I have books that cover the ins and outs of writing pitch letters and proposals.

Build on Your Strengths

While it's essential to identify where you need to improve, also look at what you are currently doing right, what you are good at, where you consistently get praise and positive feedback. This doesn't mean you can check it off your "To Be Improved" list, but it does show that you have strong skills in that area.

Why should this be part of your "raising the bar" process? By knowing what you do well, you are encouraged to keep going. You can probably remember a time when your dialogue was stilted or your articles had to undergo multiple revisions before they finally passed muster. But over the years, you have improved. Recalling progress you've made in those areas reassures you that your current weak area can also be strengthened with attention, effort and input.

Beyond the Writing

Writing is a business as well as a craft. That means that, in your ongoing quest to improve your writing skills, you don't forget the other part of living the writing life—namely, how to be a successful writer-preneur.

Do you know how to promote yourself and your work? Do you have a marketing plan for your writing business or your books—or both? What about the money side of things—which includes our less-than-favorite relative, Uncle Sam? Do you know how to track your income and expenses, what taxes you have to pay, and why you need to keep your personal and writing finances separate?

Unless you are writing only for yourself with no intention of sharing it with the rest of the world, you must have a firm grasp of the business side of things. When I decided to turn my writing abilities into an income source, I knew I needed to get some basic information if it was going to be a success. While I did start out with a bit of an advantage, having been a partner in a sales and service business for more than a decade, I didn't have a clue how to sell an intangible skill such as writing.

I stocked up on books—*Writing For Money* by Loriann Hoff Oberlin, *Secrets of a Freelance Writer* by Robert Bly, *The Freelance Writer's Handbook* by Gary Provost, *How to Open and Operate a Home-Based Writing Business* by Lucy V. Parker and *How to Start and Run a Writing & Editing Business* by Herman Holtz, among others—and devoured them. I attended conferences, signed up for seminars, and read every article I could find on the business side of being a creative professional. And over the years, I have continued to learn how to better market myself and build my business.

But when my first book, *The Gifts of Change*, came out in 2004, I was back at square one. Because I wasn't expecting to be an author, I had no firm plan for promoting my book and Nancy-the-author. So it was back to the drawing board to read books and articles on being a successful author and generating book sales. And it's still a learning process. At every writer event I attend, I reach out to other authors to discover what is working for them and how I can incorporate those strategies into my marketing while sharing with them the tips I have learned.

This is an important area of bar-raising for me. Along with always improving my writing *skills*, I have to continue to develop my writing *platform* if I want to sell more books. I have to improve my marketing skills if I want a steady income. And all this requires that I continually evaluate my progress and the strategies I'm using so that I may keep those that are working, jettison those that have failed to produce results, and find new ones that will be more effective.

If you need to "raise the bar" on your business abilities, take advantage of all the great resources available on the internet. For example, The Well-Fed Writer website has teleseminars, an e-newsletter and a knowledge base section that covers an extensive range of topics on aspects of the commercial writing business.

Both The Creative Penn and Make a Living Writing are chockful of resources. Search online and you're bound to find even more resources. And in the spirit of unity and generosity, when you figure out how to do something more effectively or efficiently, share that knowledge with other writers!

IT'S ALL ABOUT CONNECTIONS

"Writing is a lonely and isolating business."
Caitlin Kelly

Ah, peace and quiet… It's the writer's dream. No one—not boss nor friend nor family member—disturbing your creative time with phone calls, emails or in-person visits.

For most of us, that's our goal but, sadly, rarely our reality. And when we do have those golden moments of solitude, we wonder why they are so hard to come by and envy those who have undisturbed hours to devote to their writing.

But there is a flip side to that much-envied situation. Speaking as one who lives alone *and* works alone, I have to say there are times when seclusion can be too much of a good thing. It's a problem that author and writer Caitlin Kelly also struggles with.

"I don't have children or pets, so it really can be a lonely work-life if I don't leave the apartment," she said. "I make a deliberate effort to create a fairly active social life, attend professional events and go to the gym several times a week. I use social media a lot to chat with friends worldwide daily—via Facebook and Twitter—and that helps. But only talking to other writers isn't enough; it can feel too competitive and repetitive."

Author Kerin Freeman noted "you won't find a better place to write without distraction" than writing in isolation, but she also admitted that the writing life "can be a lonely existence, since having to conjure up another version of reality with believable characters and plots is all consuming."

And that can be true even if the project you're working on is nonfiction: an essay, poem or article. It's just you and your thoughts, and for every time that you are happy to be alone to pursue your creative path, there are probably ten more times when you wish there were someone else there that you could talk with, complain to or get feedback from.

But that "someone" has to be the *right* "someone." Not everyone will understand how you can agonize over a plot point or struggle with satisfying the content needs of a difficult client. Not everyone will be able to empathize when the rejections come or appreciate why an acceptance from a non-paying but prestigious market can fill your heart with joy. And not everyone will be able to comprehend what drives you to spend so many hours writing when you have no guarantee that anyone will ever read what you wrote.

Who *will* understand? Other writers, of course. They get it when you talk of the joy of completion, and they get it equally when you moan of the failure to reach a wholly satisfying conclusion.

Interacting with other writers not only has psychological benefits but also practical ones. You find out the best way to pitch your project, solicit new clients or market your book concepts. You learn what's working with your current piece—and what isn't. You discover new forms of writing and better ways of expressing your thoughts.

Jessica Strawser, author and editorial director of *Writer's Digest* magazine, recommended building a diverse writing community around yourself as one of the top three tips for success. (The other two are read a lot and write a lot!). What does she mean by "diverse"?

Include three levels of writers, she explained, "those who've achieved more success than you, those who are approximately on your own level (whatever that may be), and those who are more novice (even a kid who loves writing counts). Every writer needs a tribe, and if you assemble yours in this way you'll learn something from them all and give in return—you'll have a mentor and be a mentor, you'll gain a friend and be a friend, you'll be challenged and inspired, you'll commiserate and celebrate together."

And where do you find other like-minded souls with whom to "commiserate and celebrate"? At writing groups, conferences and writing retreats.

Writing Groups

Back in early 2012, I found myself in dire need of some "writer interaction." I wanted to meet with other writers and talk about our craft, share stories and gain feedback. But how to do it? It wasn't like I could look up "lonely writers support group" in the classifieds! So I started by finding a place where such a group could meet and, once a local coffee shop expressed its willingness to host a monthly meeting for a nominal sum, sent out a press release inviting area writers to the inaugural meeting of the Monday Night Writers. Five years later, our group is still going strong, sharing our successes and disappointments, giving and getting critiques on our works-in-progress, and, most importantly, allaying our fears that we will never achieve success, however each one of us defines it.

As writer Anita Gorman explained, being part of Monday Night Writers "has given me what I most needed: the motivation to produce one or more stories each month. But it's done more than that. From the group I learned about an essay contest that led to one of my pieces being published in an anthology, and I found out about National Novel Writing Month, a project I have participated in for the last three years. Through another member of our group, I heard about a local play-writing contest, and I was off and running. The group's members are friendly and helpful, and it's always worthwhile to listen to what others have been writing. Most of all, the group continues to give me what I initially wanted: motivation."

For author Cliff Protzman, another long-time member of the group, the feedback he received for one of his pieces led to some major editing. "I read a short story to the group that I planned to enter in an anthology contest of real life stories. The story was a personal, heartfelt memoir from my childhood. The group almost unanimously trashed it," he recalled. "The suggestions were constructive, and accurate; forcing me to look at the piece objectively. Based on their recommendations, I completely rewrote the story and entered the contest. The revised version was a winner and published in the anthology."

He added, "The image of a lonely writer hunched over a keyboard in solitude is a myth. As an author, we cannot exist in a vacuum; our tales need the vibrancy of life. A story takes on a new life when it is removed from the isolation of a computer hard drive. Active participation in a writers group is an excellent forum to expand our understanding for the art of writing. A regular meeting with a group will afford an opportunity to share works-in-progress with contemporaries. A group shares the story and enthusiastically becomes a partner. They want it to succeed and share the joy when it does. Every meeting, the members eagerly wait for the new works to be shared. Our written words are enriched by the verbal reviews."

While writer Barbara Routen noted that she enjoys "the solitude of writing and have always preferred to spend an hour researching something rather than make a 10-minute phone call asking for help," she added, "I can't be a writer if I don't experience enough of life to have material to write! Attendance at writers' groups, conferences and the monthly National League of American Pen Women meetings gives me coveted time with others in related fields. I also schedule regular get-togethers with family and friends, so, although I'm alone when I write, I work at not being a lonely writer."

Some writers establish regular writing sessions where the goal is to write together but independently—no feedback sessions and no talking, just writing. It can be the best of both worlds: you are free to work without being interrupted but the presence of the other writers dispels the sense of isolation.

In "Writing Groups 101: How to Find Your Perfect Match" on the Write Life website, writer and editor Kristen Pope provided useful ways to evaluate writing groups as well as start your own. She wrote that "having a good, solid group of writers to offer encouragement, support, and critiques can be invaluable. If there's anyone who understands what writers go through, it's other writers."

If you want the benefit of being in a writing group without the responsibility of coordinating it, ask your local bookstore or library to organize one. Or members of the group can take turns hosting the meeting. Be creative and look for ways to build your local network!

Writing Conferences and Workshops

If you've never thought about going to a writing conference or taking a writing workshop, you are missing out on a great opportunity. Attending writing conferences or signing up for a seminar can serve three purposes. The first is that the commitment of time and money reinforces your belief in yourself as a writer, not someone who is just *thinking* about writing.

Secondly, you will be among other writers at various levels of the profession. You can share your successes and fears with people who will understand what you're talking about: the terror of the blank page and the excitement of having something you wrote be accepted. You *belong*—and for many writers, being at a writing conference may be the first time they ever felt that sense of unity and kinship.

When I attended my first writing conference, the only published pieces I had were articles in my local weekly paper. Yes, I was proud of them (I had a byline, after all!), but that wasn't all I aspired to. But I doubted that my own ability would get me any higher up the publication ladder. At the conference, I heard other more experienced writers share their stories of moving from small publications to national ones, or from writing individual essays to publishing a collection.

And not all of them lived in New York or LA, knew "somebody" or in any other way had the inside track. But what they did have was the determination to keep trying, a willingness to work hard at their craft and the understanding that rejections can serve as spotlights shining on writing flaws that could be fixed. And they were equally willing to share what they knew with a "newbie" like me, giving me their contact information as well as advice on where and what to pitch.

This relationship with other writers is one you can keep alive long after the conference ends as author Josh Barkan noted. "The panels on craft, etc., are not where the real value is found. The primary value of writing conferences, such as the Association of Writing Programs annual conference, is to simply make friends with other writers—to share your own experience of writing, to realize you are not alone in the difficulties of publishing and to share your enthusiasm for writing," he said. "And as you get published, the conferences are a chance to reconnect with friends who are published writers, which sometimes also leads to opportunities such as residencies or invitations to give readings at other college campuses, etc. Your network of friends who are published writers is vital to the advancement of your career."

For Strawser, attending the 2015 Writer's Digest Conference gave her a much-needed shot in the arm. "I had just parted ways with my first agent and was unsure whether I was going to pursue another at that time, or which of my two completed novel manuscripts on my desk I wanted to submit," she recalled. "It was at the conference where I was buoyed to make the decision to move ahead with submitting my newest manuscript, which was *Almost Missed You*, though I didn't find my agent there."

In 2017, *Almost Missed You* was released by St. Martin's Press and named to the March 2017 Barnes & Noble Best New Fiction shortlist.

The third benefit comes from the talks and workshops that provide you with an education in all areas of the writing profession, from improving specific technical and creative skills to gaining an understanding of how best to market yourself and your work. Barkan had attended the Iowa Writers' Workshop and said that the experience definitely had a positive impact on his writing.

"What I learned from Frank Conroy was craft—that good writing really needs to be extremely tight and that you have a responsibility to the reader to write something that will truly interest them, to write clearly, to write with enough craft that they can enter the fictional world you create," he said. "From Jim McPherson, I learned the necessity of moral content—something truly at stake, of consequence—to make a story great."

Many writing conferences come with the added benefit of pitch sessions with agents, editors and publishers. If one of your goals is to secure an assignment, representation or a publishing contract, those face-to-face meetings can give you an edge. But to get the most out of attending a conference, you need to do some advance preparation. Review the schedule of events and choose the ones that best fit your needs and interest. Then assemble what materials you'll bring and how you're going to promote yourself and your work, especially since opportunities can arise unexpectedly.

I learned this the hard way when I went to the Willamette Writers Conference one year as both a presenter and an attendee, with two agent pitch sessions scheduled for my second book-in-progress—a self-help project featuring experts in various fields. But when the first agent asked for the names of contributors to the book I was pitching, I drew a blank. A big fat one. One the size of the largest glacier you can imagine. I couldn't remember one single name.

Then, at the second pitch session, the other agent wanted to know who would be the guests on my "Take Charge of Your Life" radio show—a major part of my platform. While I had all the names (including some high-profile celebrities and medical experts) nicely laid out on an Excel grid, I had neglected to take the basic step of printing it out. What happened? You guessed it. I drew another blank.

Shame on me for wasting such valuable opportunities. I should have known better. I *did* know better. It was just that, being so focused on my "presenter persona" and what I needed to bring for handouts, I overlooked the very obvious fact that I was *also* there to sell my own projects to those I hoped would be interested "buyers."

In her "9 tips for squeezing more out of a writers' conference" post on her WordCount: Freelancing in the Digital Age blog, journalist and editor Michelle Rafter wrote, "Stretch yourself by attending sessions on topics you think you might want to know more about." Rafter recommended leaving yourself plenty of net-working time, too, since, "it's a big part of going to a conference. Talk to people you don't know. Do more networking than you think you need to—you never know where it might lead. You could end up doing a book project with someone you had coffee with, or hiring a writer you met over drinks for the freelance editing gig you just landed."

Be ready to take notes about whom you met, what they do and how you can stay in touch. If they give you a business card, jot down the information on the back. And speaking of cards, get some yourself. They are relatively inexpensive and worth the investment. Picture this scenario: You meet a magazine editor to whom you want to pitch an idea. The two of you exchange a few words, then you mention your background and that you have some ideas that fit the publication's readership.

The editor responds, "Great! Send them along!" You thank her and make a mental note to follow up. But by the time you get back home, polish your pitches and email them to her, chances are she has met dozens of other writers and barely remembers who you are and what the two of you talked about.

Now, picture *this* scenario: You meet a magazine editor to whom you want to pitch an idea. After the two of you exchange a few words, you mention your background and that you have some ideas that fit the publication's readership. The editor responds, "Great! Send them along!"

You thank her and then, before she moves on to the next writer, you hand her a card with your name, full contact information (phone *and* email), your website or other online address where she can obtain more information about you-the-writer, and a short tag line that highlights your specialty: "freelance health writer," for example. On the back of it you add a quick note: "We met at the Ohio Writing Conference 5/10/17."

When you send your pitches, you mention the card you gave her and where you met. She may have already looked you up online, but even if she hasn't, you're establishing that the two of you had an interaction and she asked for your ideas. A small thing, maybe, but sometimes small things can have a big impact.

If you have pitch sessions scheduled with an agent or publisher, bring along plenty of information. In addition to a one-page synopsis and short bio, have the following: chapter titles and summaries, names of contributors (if applicable), and a short list of your marketing and PR plans (your platform-building activities) as well as information about your previous books. Make sure each handout has your full contact information, and have enough copies so you can provide them to each prospect.

While some people you meet may prefer that you email the information so they don't have to lug around all that paperwork, others might want the chance to review it on their way home. You can also go the digital route, putting all the details on a flash drive and offer that option as well.

In her website post, "How To Choose A Writing Conference," author and editor Erika Dreifus uses the 5Ws and 1H to outline everything you need to know to maximize your conference experience, from understanding the conference's purpose and focus to determining your reasons for attending. Take the time to analyze each conference you are considering to make sure it's a good fit for where you are as a writer and what you want to gain from it.

Writing Retreats

Writing retreats are dual-purpose experiences. Along with workshops, feedback sessions and talks, attendees also have private writing time where they can work on their projects. This can be a real boon for those who struggle with personal or professional obligations when on their home turf or who may lack the discipline to sit down and write when free time is available. Somehow, being surrounded by other writers hard at work makes it almost impossible to pick up a magazine or turn on the television.

Several times a year, author, artist, and creativity coach Claudia Taller hosts writing retreats in the northeast Ohio area. "I started doing writing retreats because I think that we create more energy and enthusiasm when we're writing together and it felt like a mission for me to be the one to make it happen," she explained. "I hope the retreat attendees give themselves permission to write their hearts out during the course of a weekend, to learn more about the craft and business of writing by being with other writers, and to participate in workshops that will strengthen and deepen their writing."

She pointed out that, for those who are considering a retreat, it's essential to evaluate "what they need from the weekend and whether the retreat format will meet their needs. I'm at the point in my career where I'm tired of hearing about how to write—I just want to do it. We can spend lots of time going to conferences and hearing the same thing over and over again, but the best way to learn how to write is to do it."

Social Media

Even if you don't know *anybody*—even if you are living in the literary equivalent of the back of beyond—it doesn't mean that you can't make your own connections and create your own breaks. The beauty of social media is that it allows you to follow (note I said, "follow," not "stalk"!) editors, agents, publishers, bloggers and other writers and share in the conversation.

I'll be the first to admit that I came late to the social media party, and my first attempts made me feel like a wallflower at the high school dance. But little by little, I became more comfortable with it, "liking" posts that I agreed with and commenting on the ones when I had something useful to offer.

One of the first things I noticed in all those virtual water-cooler talks is how often other writers bemoaned their rejections or expressed their frustration with a project they were working on. I realized that I wasn't the only person who got a "thanks, but no thanks" email from an agent or "not really what we wanted" from an editor. And once I understood that, I was able to better handle those setbacks, looking at them not as a total condemnation of my writing ability but simply as an answer to my question: "Do you want this?"

In short, whether you build virtual relationships, in-person affiliations or some combination of both, making connections with other writers not only can help offset the loneliness that plagues all of us from time to time but also give you invaluable information and advice to help you move along on your writing journey.

THE MONEY ISSUE

"The free-lance writer is a man who is paid per piece or per word or perhaps." Robert Benchley

I f you've been in the writing profession for any length of time, you most likely have been challenged by two diametrically opposed aspects of this career choice:

- On the one hand, you want to let your right brain explore new avenues, create new realities, follow where the Muse leads.

- On the other, you need to take a logical, left-brain approach to the business, weighing the income potential of each project and taking a hardline approach to questionable opportunities despite every gray cell on the right side of your head screaming, "This is a great chance! Are you out of your mind? Take it, you fool!"

So how do you reconcile those warring factions in your head? First, by deciding what role money is to play in your decision-making process. Does the profit potential of a project factor into the choice you're making? Do you care more about the prestige associated with being published in that magazine than about the amount of money you may receive? Does the assignment fit into your overall business plan, making it the right move even though from an income perspective it might be a loss?

Not all opportunities will be judged on the same scale, nor should they be. For example, writing is my profession. It's how I make my living and pay my bills. That means that the work I do—articles for magazines and copy for clients—is for monetary compensation. For this category, I have established a rate of remuneration that, for the most part, I adhere to.

But I also write essays and fiction—what I call my "passion writing." For this category, money isn't the determining factor when it comes to choosing where to submit my work. Instead, I may base my decision on the reputation of the publication or my desire to share a specific piece with the public.

Most of my published short stories have not earned me a dime, let alone a decent hourly rate for the work I put into them. But they do help build my reputation as a fiction writer, which is something money can't buy. So I don't have a problem when the "pay" comes in copies or a permanent place on the lit mag's website.

But ask me to write an article or handle content writing for a corporate client for free and my answer is a firm and unequivocal "No." I know my worth in that realm and have no intention of giving away my skills for free.

That is where I am after more than thirty years in the business. But it's been a long, hard slog to get to the point where "No" was a response I was comfortable giving—a problem that many other writers struggle with.

As writer and editor Manjula Martin put it in her book, *Scratch: Writers, Money, and the Art of Making a Living*, "In every stage of their careers, working writers are in a constant state of negotiation: work and life, art and commerce, writing and publishing… authors are said to practice a calling… but rarely a job. We are often told by more successful writers to 'do it for the love,' but we are rarely told how to turn love into a living."

What is it about associating money with writing that generates such discomfort? Why do we have such a difficult time setting a dollar value on our work as though somehow in doing so, we are degrading its artistic worth? Or is it that, since writing comes relatively easily to us (compared to the non-writers out there), we believe we shouldn't charge the industry rate—or, for that matter, "talk money" at all?

Either of the above can come into play, which can lead to the following scenario:

You contact an editor or potential copywriting client to offer your services. The prospect says, "I've reviewed your clips and background and think you'd be perfect for this project. I need 2,000 words by next week. Can you do it?" After a few mental high-fives, you respond, "Absolutely! Thanks so much! I look forward to working with you!"

What's missing from the conversation? The topic of payment: specifically, how much you'll be paid, when you are going to receive it and whether the terms are acceptable.

"But if I ask that or start negotiating, they might change their mind!" you protest. "They might think my focus is just on getting paid!"

Well, guess what—to a large extent, it is *and should be*. While you do, of course, want to turn in a well-written piece that satisfies that client or editor, you also want to be paid for your time. *And there is nothing wrong with that.*

If you were hired to clean out a drain, paint a house or repair a damaged driveway, you'd expect to be paid for your work. If you were a doctor, a lawyer or an accountant, you'd expect to be paid for your expertise. Why is writing any different?

For some of you, it might have to do with where you are in your writing career. When I first started writing for magazines and newspapers, I was so thrilled with having my work accepted that I honestly didn't care about the money.

Plus, I didn't see myself as an actual "professional writer." Even though I was good at what I did, it never occurred to me to check what the going rate was for a 2,000-word article or to ask when the check would be cut. All that mattered was that the editor said it passed muster. And if I received a compliment on my work, I would downplay my skills by explaining, "I just like to write."

When I added copywriting for clients and agencies to my list, I was still woefully ignorant of the monetary value of specific projects. All I knew was that *whatever* I was paid, it was more than the hourly rate I was earning at my regular job. And since my goal was to have enough work to allow me to freelance full time, I took any and all assignments that came my way, regardless of the amount of money.

Since then, I have learned how to ask for and get the appropriate compensation for my time and skill. And, even more importantly, when to walk away when the cost of doing business with that client or publication would exceed the income potential. I finally understood that, as much as I loved writing, it was also a business and I had to view it as such. As Billy Joel said in a 2013 *New York Times Magazine* interview, "I always had this sense that O.K., I'm an artist and I shouldn't have to be concerned about something as banal as money, which is baloney. It's my job. It's what I do."

So how do *you* get to that point? By analyzing your skill set, knowing the going rate for what you are offering, choosing your target market wisely and beefing up your negotiating skills.

Analyzing Your Skill Set

I call this starting from a Position of Power. In essence, you are identifying the writing strengths you're bringing to the bargaining table. Why is this important? Two reasons: first, when you are able to define and categorize your marketable abilities, you feel more confident about your income-earning potential.

Second, as you create this working list (and I call it a "working list" because you should always be adding to it), you recognize weak areas in your writing or missing skills that are being called for by clients and then can work to develop or enhance those proficiencies.

How do you figure out those strengths, especially if you are just getting into freelancing? Start by evaluating your past writing experience.

Have you:

- Handled writing assignments at your job where you prepared reports, developed employee manuals or wrote web copy?

- Been in charge of the publicity for a local organization or non-profit, writing press releases or content for public relations materials?

- Helped job-seeking friends or family members by drafting their résumés or CVs?

Now look at your abilities and preferences—those writing-related projects you are either good at or like to do or both. This will give you some ideas of how to translate them into marketable services.

For example:

- If you enjoy research, possibilities include community histories, directories, economic development materials, tourism guides or genealogies.

- If you have a flair for succinct and catchy phrases, options include social media posts, ad copy and direct mail materials.

- If your editing and proofreading skills are strong, you can offer them to college students who require term papers edited, writers who need an eagle eye turned on their manuscripts and agencies who are preparing copy for clients.

- If you have a strong background in a particular industry—for example, in the medical or technical arenas—your experience combined with your writing ability can be invaluable to companies in that industry who need to get their message to the appropriate market. You already know the jargon and can speak and write it fluently.

Finally, review job openings in your local paper, on employment boards like Monster.com or on LinkedIn to learn what skills, abilities, background and education are most desired. Visit websites of other freelancers to get a sense of what they are offering. You'll discover how your current strengths align with what's most in demand and identify those categories where you need to broaden your skill set.

Knowing the Going Rate

Great. You have established what you have to offer and can provide specific examples that illustrate your capabilities. But now you come down to setting a price for your services. What *is* the going rate for your writing skills?

This is an ongoing challenge, whether you are new to the business or have been in it for years. Many factors can affect your rates. Before the recession in 2007, I had a decent rate structure. But when my business clients tightened their purse strings due to the economic downturn, I had to adjust my fees to reflect their current spending limit.

At the same time, the magazine industry that had provided me with a good source of income was also affected, and I watched with no small dismay as $2-per-word assignments dropped to $1-per-word or even less. While the pay rate has been on an upswing since those dark days, the experience reinforced the importance of staying tuned into what's happening in the industries I write for and the economy in general so I'm not caught unawares and under-funded.

Another factor has to do with geography—a lesson I learned when bidding on a job for a prospect based on the West Coast. At the time, most of my corporate work came from local northeast Ohio companies, and my rates were in tune with what they were able and willing to pay. Then came a chance to submit a proposal to a California corporation for a major copywriting job. The company wanted a per-hour figure, so I gave them my regular rate and waited anxiously for the response, wondering if I should have made it even lower.

Finally, I got the word that the company had accepted my bid although, as the woman in charge of the marketing department explained, they had had some reservations about hiring me. *Not* because of my experience or work samples, but because my rate was so much lower than the rest of those submitted by copywriters in their location.

"To be honest," she said, "we wondered how good you could be if that was all you were charging."

That insight into how the perceived value of my work was tied to the fee I was charging was a game-changer for me, and I made it my business to: 1) know what the industry rate was for different writing projects and 2) be willing to walk away when the proposed compensation fell far short of what was reasonable.

A side note: Some experts have recommended that writers just starting out should offer to handle a project for free as a way of getting their foot in the door. I don't believe in that approach because it demeans what you offer. If you provide a service, *you should be paid for it.*

Here's my analogy: I have never worked in a fast-food restaurant and am pretty sure that, if I did, I wouldn't be very good at it. I'd put pickles on a no-pickle order and forget that catsup went with the fries. At the end of my first working day, I would probably be fired. *But I would still get paid for being there.*

If you aren't sure that your work is good enough, then take a class to improve your skills. But if you are confident that you can meet the client's expectations, then charge a fee. Granted, you can also do pro bono writing for organizations you belong to or want to support. That's fine. But giving away your skills for free to those clients you view as potential income sources doesn't make sense from either a financial or psychological perspective.

For one thing, you are telling them that you don't have enough confidence in your abilities to charge for them. For another, how will you transition them from non-paying clients to paying ones? This is a business. Treat it like one.

But for many writers, that can be more easily said than done. "Talking money is especially uncomfortable for women, I think, and for new independents," said writer and editor Robin Baum. "We have a tendency to undervalue what we do, and until we have proven our worth by completing projects, we don't trust ourselves. I think fear of failure also plays a role in this. There's no way around it—each of us must research pricing, choose a fair and appropriate rate for our work, and then suck it up and put it out there. Once you've billed and received your first checks, it will reinforce that you made the right decision—or not, and then you can adjust your fees."

There are some excellent online resources to provide you with typical rates for a variety of writing projects. These include the Editorial Freelancers Association (click on Resources), Profitable Copy (click on Free Estimate) and the freelance rate calculator under the Resources tab on the All Freelance Writing website. Moira Allen's website, Writing-World.com, also has a lot of valuable information in the Negotiating Contracts and Setting Fees/Getting Paid section.

Baum based her initial fees on a combination of what she learned from her local Public Relations Society of America, Inc. (PRSA) and International Association of Business Communicators (IABC) organizations about the going rates in her region. She also used the Freelance Rate Chart on the Writing Assistance, Inc. website.

"As a new independent writer/editor with extensive healthcare experience, I began at the low-mid end of the scale but planned in small annual increases," she said. "I have raised my rates each year, letting my clients know in December that the rates would go up slightly in January. No one has ever had an issue with it, I think because I'm still much less expensive than an agency overall."

But that's just the beginning of the process. Rates can be:

- Per-word: a price based on the number of words—for example, $1 per word for a 1,000-word article (more common for publications)

- Per-piece: also called flat-rate or per-project, a set sum for the finished project

- Per-hour: an hourly rate, which the client may also cap at a certain figure

- Per-page: a rate for each page of a document, commonly used for editing manuscripts

Knowing how projects are typically charged and what rate is appropriate for the work can help you set your own rates accordingly. But you'll also want to take into account your own level of experience and adjust your rates as needed, increasing them as you gain experience—a strategy that author and editor Ann Henry has followed since she opened her writing business, Ann Henry Literary Services, in 2015.

"Before I set my rates, I checked other editing services online, figured out the basic range, and set my rate in the middle of that range. Since then I have raised my rate once due to my increased costs and experience," she explained.

Henry also has two different rate structures: a standard one for her commercial clients and a reduced rate for works of fiction or for nonfiction works related to the writing of fiction. "It's my way of giving back to the writing community because it is so dear to my heart. My advice is to stand by your rates unless the client is one you wish to grant a discount for personal reasons or who is willing to assist you with valuable marketing that makes giving a discount worthwhile."

Baum does do some work at no charge, especially if it will help with getting recognition or other value in exchange. "For example, I recently facilitated a logo branding project for a local high-profile nonprofit, and worked with the CEO, the Board of Directors and a printing company president to make it happen," she said. "The collaborative effort resulted in a new relationship with a printer, a happy Board of professionals and CEO, and an award I will be receiving at their annual meeting this year."

Choosing Your Target Market

Now you're at the seek-and-pitch stage where you are looking for copywriting clients and magazine opportunities. Go back to your skills and use them as a way of categorizing the clients you want to write for. When I first started out, I had a strong background in running a small business, so I wrote many articles targeted to that readership.

I also had experience researching health issues and treatment options so added personal health and well-being to my list, writing articles for wellness publications as well as copy for hospitals. The point is, you will feel more confident if you start pitching your services to those prospects in specific industries or with needs where you have a strong level of expertise and familiarity.

You can also reach out to those companies and organizations with whom you already have a connection. Does your accountant need a writer to do the occasional press release? Does your insurance agent require a ghostwriter to draft articles for industry publications? Is there a customer with whom you've built a relationship through your current non-freelance position who has mentioned that updates to the company website are on hold because "we just can't find a writer"? These are all opportunities worth exploring.

Baum offered some additional suggestions from her own experience building her writing and editing service. "Depending on the type of writing you specialize in, you can join local chambers of commerce and network face-to-face with small businesses that need writers for specific projects but can't afford to have one on staff," she said. "Asking about their communication or marketing challenges can lead to offering ideas of how you could write or edit for them. Your business card will be kept and they will contact you later, when they realize they need your help."

She has also used speaking opportunities for local business-related nonprofits to promote her company. "Providing a presentation at no cost has often led to clients who see value in what I present and the type of work I do."

Beefing Up Your Negotiating Skills

So here you are, at the bargaining table. The prospective client has just outlined the project parameters and given you the budget—a budget, by the way, that you know is less than what it should be, given the time and expertise required.

What do you do? Do you sigh internally and say, "Okay, I can do it for that," following the "bird-in-the-hand" axiom? Or do you negotiate for a better deal? And if you choose the latter course of action, how exactly does that work?

Carol Tice, nonfiction author and ghostwriter, learned about the art of negotiation from her experience years earlier working at a Hollywood studio. At the time, she was a legal secretary for an attorney in the television department who handled negotiations for actor contracts within a very tight deadline, often overnight. When the stack of contracts would land on his desk, he would spend hours hammering out a deal with the agents that was acceptable to both sides.

"The back-and-forth went on for hours since none of the actors accepted the original offers," said Tice. "Know what I learned from this experience? Negotiating is normal. I'll say it again. Negotiating. Is. Normal. It's what businesspeople do. Keep it friendly, give and take, and you can negotiate and get more of what you want."

I like to use a combination of the "pregnant pause" and "wiggle words" when I am negotiating a rate for a project. After I have asked all my questions about the assignment—when it's due and what the parameters are—I ask what the budget is. If the figure and terms the client quotes me are acceptable, we have a deal. Otherwise, I say, "Oh," and pause.

This not only gives me time to decide whether I want to accept the rate but also tells the client that I am thinking it over. And since people, like nature, abhor a vacuum, the person may fill the empty conversational space by saying, "But we can go a little higher and/or pay a little faster" or in some other way offer a pot-sweetener that will make it worth it.

The qualifying phrase comes into play when a client asks what my rate is, either for a specific project or in general. Often, I have no way of knowing what they have paid freelance writers in the past, but I do know what my acceptable rate range is.

So I say something like, "Generally speaking, for a project like this, I usually charge $X." The wiggle words "generally speaking" and "usually" give me the option of adjusting (i.e., wiggling) my rate based on the situation: "But since you need a 24-hour turn-around, I'd have to charge more" or "But since you are a local non-profit and I know your budget is tight, I'm willing to reduce it a bit" or something similar.

This four-part strategy—analyzing your skill set, knowing the going rate for what you are offering, choosing your target market wisely and beefing up your negotiating skills—will make it easier for you to have that "money talk" with clients and editors.

After all, being a writer is not only a calling—for many of us, it's an occupation as well. It's a way to earn a living, pay our bills and provide for our future and those we share our life with.

Author and journalist Larry Kahaner put it succinctly in his post "If You Insist on Having Writer's Block, Here's Help" on his

The Non-Fiction Novelist blog: "Professional writers don't have muses; they have mortgages." Those mortgages and all the other financial obligations we have require cold hard cash to satisfy. And how we satisfy them is with our writing skills.

Remember, someone, somewhere out there, needs what you offer. All you have to do is find that one person and demonstrate that your creative ability and writing skills are just what is required. And just as importantly, know what your compensation should be and believe that you are worth what you are charging.

After you get to that point, do all that is reasonable to maintain that writer-client relationship. You've put a lot of time and effort into shifting that person, editor or company from a potential customer to a "signed on the dotted line" one. Now you need to make sure it remains a mutually beneficial situation, and you do that by building the relationship.

Building Relationships

While money matters in business transactions, so does building relationships. Ideally, clients or editors will stay with you for years, giving you regular assignments. But that only happens if: 1) they are happy with your work and 2) they are happy with *you*. Your writing may be Pulitzer Prize caliber, but if your attitude is less than friendly and your reliability measures on the low end of the scale, they may decide you are more trouble than you're worth.

If you want to keep those clients on your "active list," then do everything you can to meet their expectations—and then some, recommended Baum. "Professional courtesy with editors and clients will take you far. By that, I mean politeness and extra communication, and providing more than they ask for each time—e.g., getting content to them early when possible, and providing images or other files before they ask for them," she said.

"It takes time to build good relationships, but they will last once they are built," she stressed. "Frequent communication is important, but building a relationship based on providing quality content on time every time is even more critical. It will build loyalty and allow you to negotiate new projects or fees when you need to. Promise realistically and over-deliver, and you'll be in a great position to negotiate in the future."

"THANKS, BUT NO THANKS"

"Rejection is difficult but you can always learn something from an editor's or publisher's response, even a negative one." **Q.L. Pearce**

Those darned rejection letters. We've all gotten them from publishers or agents, editors or clients, telling us, in one way or another, that we just aren't good enough. Or at least, that's how we perceive them. Isaac Asimov, quoted in Aerogramme Writers' Studio's "12 Famous Writers on Literary Rejection," referred to them as "lacerations of the soul, if not quite inventions of the devil."

And sometimes, when you get a series of them over several days (or even worse, multiple ones in a single day!), it can feel like death by a thousand emails—negative ones, that is.

While there's no denying that an acceptance letter is far more desirable than one saying "thanks, but no thanks," there are ways you can deal with the negative responses to keep you from sinking into that black hole of despair while enabling you to gain something from the experience.

The first is to understand that everyone receives them: the first-time writer *and* the well-known one. Many of those first-timers went on to achieve publishing success *because they didn't let the rejections stop them*!

Don't believe me? Check out Writer's Relief's "Famous Author Rejection Letters: True Stories Of Unbelievable Rejections."

Among those listed in the article are the rejections received by Sylvia Plath ("There certainly isn't enough genuine talent for us to take notice") and Rudyard Kipling ("I'm sorry Mr. Kipling, but you just don't know how to use the English language"). As for not giving up after the first, second or tenth rejection, the article noted the following authors who raised determination to an art form: James Lee Burke (111 rejections), Robert Pirsig (121 rejections), and Jack Canfield and Mark Victor Hansen (134 rejections).

As Catherine Wald wrote in the introduction to her book, *The Resilient Writer: Tales of Rejection and Triumph by 23 Top Authors*, "Persistence can pay off. More than one of the authors in this book was rejected by every MFA program in the country. Some have collected literally hundreds of rejection slips."

Those are the facts of the writing life, true for authors seeking publication for their books as well as for those who write copy for corporate clients or articles for magazines. There are always going to be more "Thanks, but no thanks" than "Let's move forward with this book/contract/piece."

But just because the odds favor rejection doesn't mean you should give up. More importantly, wrote Wald, remember that it's always your choice how to handle those negative responses. "If you let rejection, despair, or confusion make you quit, that's your choice. You also have the option of choosing to write, no matter what."

An article in a newsletter from Mridu Khullar Relph, freelance journalist, author and founder of The International Freelancer website, really struck home with me. In "Is rejection your fault? Or theirs?" she talked about the rejection letters she had received from literary agents for her first novel before she secured representation.

She wrote, "I read the rejection letters, some very kind, others indifferent, and sure, my tiny lacking-in-confidence writer heart weeps a little. I might sulk for an hour or two. I tell myself that I'm a terrible writer and that there's no reason for me to believe that my work is anything other than personal gratification. Then I have a small piece of chocolate (or three) and the pragmatic part of me gets into gear. It says, look, if I'm terrible at this, then the only way to not be so terrible is to practice and keep writing in order to get better. And if I work on the next book, then even if this one doesn't sell, I won't be the failure, this particular book will."

In her essay, "Why You Should Aim for 100 Rejections a Year" on the Literary Hub website, writer Kim Liao shared a strategy she got from a writer friend who, she noted, had "impressive rates of acceptance." Liao wrote, "I asked her what her secret was, and she said something that would change my professional life as a writer: 'Collect rejections. Set rejection goals. I know someone who shoots for one hundred rejections in a year, because if you work that hard to get so many rejections, you're sure to get a few acceptances, too.'"

I wish *I* had gotten that advice when I first started submitting my short stories. When I initially started sending out my fiction, it was a long, arduous process. I would spend hours perusing *Writer's Market* at my local library, looking for a market that might possibly want my work. Then I would type up the story, check it for errors, re-type it (I was and still am a terrible typist!) and put it into an envelope with the obligatory SASE. (This was back when submissions were done via snail-mail.)

And then I would wait. And wait. And wait.

And while I was waiting, I wouldn't even consider submitting a *different* story to a *different* market, even though I had plenty more in my file cabinet ready to go.

Maybe I thought that by submitting a second story I was saying I believed Story Number One wasn't good enough and so this was my back-up. Or maybe I didn't think *anything* I wrote was good enough to get accepted, so that by only sending out one, I was reducing the number of rejections I would ultimately receive.

In any case, months would go by until I received the rejection letter or got no letter at *all* and had to face the fact that no one wanted my story or, by extension, me. It would take me several more months to screw up my courage and try again, with the same results. When I finally received an acceptance letter, I couldn't believe it. I was sure the editor had made a mistake, that it was intended for some other Nancy Christie who had submitted a story with the same title. It wasn't until I actually saw the magazine with my byline under the story title that I believed it!

Since then I have logged close to 400 submissions to literary markets. (The number is a little fuzzy because I didn't log the early ones—didn't want to remember them, I guess!) Including the ones that are in my short story collection, *Traveling Left of Center and Other Stories*, only 33 have been accepted. Now, math isn't my strong point, but I am reasonably certain my percentage of successful submissions is low. Really, *really* low.

But, despite the mathematical probability of receiving a rejection, I keep doing it, albeit now without having to resort to typing manuscripts, licking envelope flaps and sticking on stamps. (Thank you, online submission managers!) Of course, the wait is still excruciatingly slow, but I fill my time by, you guessed it, submitting more. And writing more. And submitting those new ones as soon as they are completed and pass muster.

What I have learned in the decades since I first started sending out my work is to accept that rejections, if not welcome, are at least to be expected. "Rejections are inevitable, especially as publication becomes more and more competitive. Even very talented writers are turned down again and again," said author Patricia Averbach.

"But doesn't a rejection mean the piece was no good?" you ask. Not necessarily, and I go back to my spreadsheet for proof. I've had work that was accepted by the first market I sent it to, and stories that were rejected more than 20 times before finding a home—and lots of praise. I have also received rejection letters that were complimentary about the piece but said it just wasn't the right fit. (Yes, that *could* be the standard form letter content, but when an editor adds a comment that specifically praises some part of the story or your writing in general, take it as the truth!)

And while I have received the form letter rejection as well— lots of them!—spending my time wondering what it was about the submission that didn't make the cut would, for the most part, be a fruitless endeavor. If I did my homework and picked the right market, knew my story was written to the best of my ability and submitted it according to the publication's rules, then it was, to a large extent, a purely subjective decision by the editor.

Not that knowing that fact makes the rejection easier to take! As author Christopher Klein said, "It's never easy to get turned down, particularly when you are shopping around book proposals. You sink so much time into putting together a book proposal and you think it's a great idea. It's really hard to hear from publishers that they don't see the same value in the idea that you do. It's important to keep in mind, however, that being a writer is similar to being a baseball player. Even the greatest baseball hitters fail more than six out of every ten times at the plate. Focus on the successes, not the failures."

But sometimes keeping that focus can be difficult, especially when it appears that you are hearing "You're out!" (to stay with the baseball analogy) more often than not. That walk back to the dugout, i.e., your writing space, can seem like a painful, interminable journey.

"The pain of rejection is hard-wired into our brains," said Wald. "In the good old caveman days, she who was cast out by the tribe was likely to die. So we have reasons to fear and hate rejection. Everyone hates it, and while it may get easier over time, it never gets easy. Those who have made their peace with it enjoy their writing and their lives a whole lot more. And people who have succeeded in their writing careers or their practices as writers are the ones who have learned to take all rejections with many grains of salt and to continue writing."

Refuse to let those negative responses stop you from submitting. Actually, the more balls you have in the air (meaning, submissions in the queue), the less upset you are when one falls to the floor (you get a rejection). I take to heart William Zinsser's advice, as quoted in *The Resilient Writer*, to not waste time crying (or complaining) about the "no" answer but to send it back out

ASAP in hopes of getting a "yes." And then I start working on another piece.

That's the same strategy followed by author and writer Kelly Boyer Sagert. As she explained, "What has always worked for me is to have multiple projects going on so when one fails, it's not the end of the world. Even if it was really a big one, something that I really wanted to work, as long as I have enough irons in the fire, I'm able to keep going."

Here's what you have to understand and accept: rejection is part and parcel of the writer's life.

- If you are a copywriter, there will be times when the client for whom you have just written a stellar piece of copy will complain, "It's not what I wanted."

- If you write magazine articles, there will be times when the editor will send it back with critical comments in the margin and a request for "a revision by tomorrow morning: better sources, better quotes, better content."

- If you write essays or fiction, there will be times when the publication will reject the piece with the aforementioned form letter or, if you're lucky, some explanation that supports the decision.

And if you write books—and writing a *good* book, fiction or nonfiction, is a long, laborious and at times frustrating experience!—you are looking at two possible outcomes for your pitches. One is a flat-out "thanks, but no thanks" from the literary agent or acquisitions editor. Alternatively, if it's accepted, expect a requirement for editorial changes that run the gamut from requesting a new title to eliminating whole chapters while adding new ones.

You also must decide whether the requested changes would improve the work or take it in a direction that you don't like or that you don't think will fit the piece. Author Q.L. Pearce said,

"I have a friend who almost sold a novel to a major publisher but they wanted her to write out an important character. She decided against it. Not long after, she sold that same novel to a different publisher who thought the character in question was fabulous. Her book did very well and is still in print. I think the bottom line is to listen to advice but write the story you want to tell."

So, given that the negative responses will undoubtedly far outweigh the positive ones, how can you learn to handle them effectively? What can you take from them to improve your writing and perfect your submission process while you keep on submitting?

My suggestion, developed after years (and years and years) of submitting fiction, essays, articles and book pitches, is to follow the "3 Ws" strategy: Who, What and When.

Who

The "who" is the person you addressed your query or submission to, and this is important because nothing turns off a recipient faster than receiving a letter or email addressed to the wrong person. Or to "Ms." when he's a "Mr." While it's true that some publications don't provide a person's name but tell you to send it to the "Submissions Editor," you should make the effort to find out who that person is.

Start with the masthead, that place where all the editors are listed. (Hint: A "Contributing Editor" is *not* the person to send it to since those holding that title don't make editorial decisions.) You can also search LinkedIn or Google for the magazine to find names connected with it. While market guides can be helpful, bear in mind that people frequently change positions both within a specific publication and in the industry itself, and Bob Jones who has been the submissions editor at ABC Press might now be the executive editor at 123 Magazine.

Another interesting (and irritating!) fact: If the person is no longer there, your letter or email won't necessarily come back to you but may instead reside in some gray space between delivery and return. You will think it has gone to its destination, but it hasn't, and in the meantime you are losing the chance to send it where it needs to go. That makes it even more important to do the best you can to ensure your send-to address is a working one.

Writing-related newsletters and websites are other sources you can turn to for up-to-date information. Some of my favorites are the *Writer's Digest* weekly e-newsletter, Tara Lynne Groth's "Write Naked", "The ASJA Weekly", C. Hope Clark's "Funds for Writers", New Pages and Angela Hoy's "Writers Weekly".

This is also where your writing network can be very useful. I have reached out to writers for names of editors, agents and publishers and have received great insider's info: what that person was like to work for, how the agent or publisher responded (if at all!) and what the overall outcome was like. Writing conferences can be a goldmine of contacts since many have industry professionals on their list of presenters. (Can't attend a conference? Check out the conference website where information about those who are speaking or doing workshops is available.)

What

Okay, you've got the "who" figured out. Now it's time to look at the "what"; namely, what exactly you are sending.

While each target will have its specific guidelines, there are some general rules. For articles, put together a pitch letter including details about the topic, the sources and any other relevant information about the subject and yourself—for example, your writing credits or familiarity with the topic. Nonfiction book? A solid proposal together with a couple of chapters. A short story, essay or novel? The finished piece, please!

What you are submitting should match both your target's submission format and its preferences. Don't send horror stories to literary magazines featuring romances. Don't send how-to articles to publications that have never included them in their issues. Don't pitch an adult crime novel to a literary agent whose bio clearly states her preferences for YA (young adult) material.

In her book, *What Editors Want: A Must-Read for Writers Submitting to Literary Magazines*, editor and author Lynne Barrett wrote, "Remember the editor's deepest wish: Send something perfect for us, please. So your job is to help the editor by sending work that is developed, complete, thoroughly revised, polished, and—of great importance—appropriate for the magazine. To do that last part of your job well, you have to read the magazines."

Just as important is to follow the rules on how to submit the piece. Is it to be sent by email, snail-mail or via an online submission format? Do you need to strip out all identifying information so it's a "blind" submission? Is there a submission fee you must pay?

When

When I used to snail-mail my book pitches to agents, I would take the extra step of calling first to learn if they were currently open to submissions. Now with so many literary agencies and publishers having websites, it's far easier to check on whether it's the right time to submit or if they are temporarily closed to pitches.

Literary magazines may accept submissions year-round or only have open calls during specific months. Some have periods when you can submit without paying a fee or only have a fee if you are entering your piece in a competition versus just a standard submission. Consumer magazines usually accept "evergreen" stories (those that are of interest to readers at any time, such as "10 ways to save money") year-round but have deadlines for those that are linked to specific holidays or seasons. For the latter, knowing the publication's lead time is essential, since stories dealing with Halloween may be chosen by March 1!

Handling Rejections

So you've done everything right. You picked the right target, prepared your submission according to the rules and sent it out before the deadline. And it still gets rejected. Now what?

First, said Barrett, understand that "all writers have work rejected, even writers who already have extensive publications and have won awards. There are no guarantees. Rejections primarily mean that the work doesn't suit the needs of that particular publication at that time, which happens even for very polished and meritorious work. It may have to do with whether the submission is appropriate for this particular market or the unforeseeable fact that the editor has just accepted something very similar. But it is also important to understand that editors get far more work of merit than they can use, and simply get to choose what they like best."

She added, "If the writer has done the homework of researching and reading many possible markets for the piece, then he or she will have other options lined up to send it to immediately."

It's a strategy that Barrett herself has followed over the years. "When something I've written is rejected, I generally already have other places in mind to send it to, and I will send it out again immediately unless, while it was under consideration, some particular idea for improving it has occurred to me. Overall, I keep a record of my submissions, rejections, rejections with comments or encouragement, and acceptances, so I can look back and see the journey a particular piece has taken. Of course it is sometimes disappointing, but I try to keep my mind on the big picture. The goal is to improve your average, not to bat 1000."

Wald remembered the early days when rejection letters would drive her to tears. Now, she said, "I let myself feel the pain for a brief period of time, really feel it, and maybe scream or throw something against the wall. With the release of that anger, it's a lot easier to get back to work. I try to look at every 'declined' as a badge of honor. It just makes every acceptance that much sweeter.

A big problem with our culture is that if something doesn't happen instantly, we feel like a failure and give up. I've found it really helpful to take a long-term, really long-term, approach. If you are committed to your writing and your craft, it will be a lifelong pursuit and actually a lifelong joy, too. You might as well pace yourself."

Writer Tara Lynne Groth takes a practical approach to rejections. "If it's a rejection of my creative work, I re-read and revise the story and send it to my critique group for another round of edits. Then I send the story out again."

She suggested letting the piece rest for a while before revising. "A day, a week, a month—clarity comes with time in ways you don't expect. If the rejection is for professional writing work, conduct a SWOT analysis to identify your strengths, weaknesses, opportunities and threats. Then you can develop strategies that help make you stronger and take advantage of opportunities, while minimizing threats. This might prompt you to develop niches and specialize in some areas, or make you re-focus your writing business in other ways, such as more speaking events than content writing, or more books than articles."

I have had extensive experience receiving what Wald referred to as "badges of honor" (i.e., rejection letters) although I don't follow Stephen King's example (shared in *On Writing*) of hanging the rejection letters on a nail pounded in the wall since I prefer *not* to have them so visible! However, I do maintain a submission spreadsheet. I log what I sent, when I sent it, the print or online publication I sent it to, when it came back or was accepted, and what notes (both positive or negative) accompanied the response.

If I consistently read the same critique or a suggestion for how to improve the work, sometimes I may take the advice and revise the piece. If, along with the rejections, editors ask that I send them another piece since my overall style appealed to them, I look for what to submit to them next. If the critique was more along the lines of "good writing but this piece just isn't a good fit," then I know the fault was in my choice of market, not with the piece. The important thing is that each time, I learn something. (Regarding those markets that *never* respond—not to the original submission and not to my follow-ups—I learned *not* to submit to them again!)

You would think that after authoring more than 30 books, Dawn Reno Langley would be able to turn her projects in with only a handful of revisions. But that would be wrong.

"I used to think that the third or fourth draft of a book was good enough to send out," she said. "Not anymore. Even with decades of experience under my belt, I still turned to a developmental editor for help with the last stages of the project that became *The Mourning Parade*. Even after I worked with her, I rewrote the novel four more times, adding another plot line, another point of view, and really amping up the language."

But even with all the effort, Langley still gets the occasional rejection and has to deal with the reaction that accompanies it. "I still feel like a failure when my work is rejected or when someone I thought would be a definite 'yes' comes through with a 'no,'" she admitted. "I used to give myself a night to think about it, and it was always better the next day, but now I realize that I only need one 'yes.' It may take a lot of 'no's' to get to that 'yes,' but if I don't keep sending out my work, I'll never find out."

Her advice? "Send your work out only when you've had great comments from at least three writers whose work you admire. Work hard. And when you think you're finished, put the work away for a couple of weeks, do something else, then go back into it and cut 10,000 words."

Succeeding as a writer (however you define success) means you have to be able to accept the rejection without letting it destroy your confidence and keep you from writing. As author Wally Wood said, "Being rejected by an agent (as I have been), being rejected by a magazine (too often to count), not being selected by Kindle Press (just this summer), has nothing to do with failure. My work might be rejected for many reasons apart from the actual writing, and there's nothing personal about not being selected. I just keep doing my best writing every day."

Or take the advice of Barbara Kingsolver, also from the Aerogramme Writers' Studio's article: "Don't consider it rejected. Consider that you've addressed it 'to the editor who can appreciate my work' and it has simply come back stamped 'Not at this address'."

WRITING ROADBLOCKS

*"I believe that writer's block is not the disease but
a symptom of something else: fear." Wally Wood*

So here you are, driving along the highway on your way to
your carefully planned destination, and suddenly you run
into a roadblock. Not a detour, which would at least give you
hope that, with some delay, you might reach your journey's end.
Nope, this one is a definite barricade, and as you hit the brakes
and consider what to do next, you wonder if there might have
been some way of avoiding it.

Sound familiar? This can happen not only on the asphalt
highway but on your writing highway as well. You've got your
"itinerary" (i.e., writing plan) all figured out, but somewhere along
the way you hit an obstruction, and your writing grinds to a halt.

Some writers call it "writer's block" and live in fear of its happening to them or, when it does, are terrified that the wall will be
too high to surmount. Others consider it the inevitable result of
trying to fit the demands of a creative life into the larger obligations of "real life"—something that has to be accepted and dealt
with one way or the other.

And then there are those WWs ("writer wannabes") who see
every obstacle as a message from Fate that being a writer is not
a realistic goal or a practical career objective—or maybe just too
darned hard!

Regardless of which camp you belong to (and you may visit all three from time to time!), there are ways you can overcome these setbacks with a little initiative, determination and (most uncomfortable of all) honest self-assessment.

Roadblock #1: Lack of Time

Time—sometimes *finding* time to write can be your greatest challenge. The kids are sick, the boss wants you to work late, the laundry or lawn demands attention, or you have a million other things on your plate, and *none* of them involves your writing. So how do you put your creative self *first*—or at least, get it on the list? How exactly do you *find* the time? And just as important, what is the *best* time for you?

Let's address the last question first, which involves knowing a little about circadian rhythms, those physical, mental and behavioral changes operating more or less on a 24-hour cycle. In his *Harvard Business Review* article, "The Ideal Work Schedule, as Determined by Circadian Rhythms," writer Christopher M. Barnes talked about morning people or "larks" whose ebb and flow of alertness start earlier than for most people—a category that I fall into.

While I can edit, revise and research any time of day, that initial creation stage goes the best if I do it early in the morning, preferably when the robins are just waking up and the sun is starting to burn away the night. Other people do their best writing mid-day, in the evening or late at night after everyone else has gone to bed.

And then there are writers like Julie Anne Lindsey who operate on the "any time I can find the time" schedule. While she said she does her best work in the morning, Lindsey's writing schedule spans morning to night-time.

"Monday through Friday, I write from 5:30 to 6:30 AM (until the kids' school buses begin to come), then 8:30 to 3 PM (while they're in school), then 9 PM to midnight (after they're in bed and until I faceplant on my keyboard)," she said. "On my weekends,

I only write when the family is asleep or otherwise engaged, so … morning from 5:30 to 9, then after 10 PM." She added, "My brain gets tired as the day goes on, but you've got to do what you've got to do and sometimes that means late night writing and extensive early morning revisions."

A side note: Know those brilliant ideas or solutions to a plot issue that strike just when you're falling asleep? According to writer Elena Bajic in her *Forbes* article, "How To Achieve Peak Productivity Levels, Even While Procrastinating," you can thank your fatigue for that. The article cited a study from the journal *Thinking & Reasoning* that found "tasks involving creativity might benefit from a non-optimal time of day." In other words, while being tired or groggy might not be the best time to edit, it can help you do some out-of-the-box literary problem-solving!

Chances are, there are periods in the day when your creativity engine is firing on all cylinders. Note when that occurs, which can help you as you schedule your writing time. And you *must* schedule it, otherwise it isn't going to happen. In his book, *The Seven Habits of Highly Effective People*, Stephen Covey stressed the importance of scheduling your priorities. But before you can do that, you need to know what they are or, as he put it, what is the "yes" burning inside you that overshadows all else.

If having time to write—if writing itself—is as important as you say it is, then it belongs on your schedule. And to get it on the schedule, you need to remove something else. It's not about *finding* more time but in making better use of the time you *have*. Like everyone else, you have the same 24 hours and the same 1440 minutes each day. It's your decision as to how you use it.

I can hear you now: "Easy for you to say, but this project requires a huge chunk of time—entire weeks, at least! And I can't devote that kind of time to it with everything else I have to do!"

You're right. You probably can't. If you're like most writers, your time is stretched so thin you can see through it. So forget about trying to set aside those days or weeks and start with minutes—30 minutes to be exact—using my "30 in 30" technique.

It's simple and only requires that you commit to spending 30 minutes a day writing for the next 30 days. Now to do that, you need to find that half-hour in the 24 hours that make up each day.

I know—you're going to say you don't have time to do this. And perhaps you don't—at least, the way your life is organized right now. But think about it: if a friend or family member needed you for 30 minutes a day for the next 30 days, you'd find a way to find the time. If your boss said you had to stay late for 30 minutes for the next 30 days, you'd find a way to find the time.

Isn't your writing worth that 30-minute/30-day commitment?

Let's look for some places where you can find that golden half-hour:

- Can you give up a TV show, cut back on your telephone conversations, bribe the kids or your spouse to take over a household task?

- Can you get up a little earlier or go to bed a little later?

- Can you write while you eat your lunch or wait for the clothes to finish at the Laundromat?

- Can you use the time during your commute—a strategy that had been used by novelists John le Carré, Peter Brett, Jonathan Stone and Peter King?

Thirty minutes isn't very much time to find *if* you make a determined effort to locate it. You would be amazed at what you can do with just a relatively small time commitment!

What else do you need to do to ensure success? Write it in your day planner or enter it into your online calendar, just like you would with any other can't-miss appointment. This is *your* time to write—no matter what.

Then make a public announcement. Tell everyone who could possibly interfere with your schedule that you are *not* to be disturbed because you need this time to write. Why the big announcement? Two reasons: first, to avoid the "But you didn't tell me you had this planned" conversation with your nearest and dearest, and second, because now that you made such a big deal out of it, you have to do it.

Next, pick your writing spot and get it ready to go. You don't want to waste a single second of your thirty minutes looking for the power cord or a sharp pencil or a working desk lamp. (By the way, all those items that you say you must have before you start writing—do you *really* need them or are you just procrastinating?)

Finally, on Day One, plant yourself in that place for 30 minutes. Use a timer if necessary to keep you from quitting ahead of schedule. (It's amazing how long 30 minutes can seem when you aren't making any progress!) You might just sit there, staring at the paper or monitor, and wonder why you are putting yourself through this. Or you write a few sentences, maybe even a few paragraphs, and then realize what you produced is so bad it isn't even worth saving.

That's okay. That's even to be expected. You aren't the only writer who gets stuck at the starting gate. Lawrence Block said, "One thing that helps is to give myself permission to write badly. I tell myself that I'm going to do my five or 10 pages no matter what, and that I can always tear them up the following morning if I want. I'll have lost nothing—writing and tearing up five pages would leave me no further behind than if I took the day off."

If you stick with it, if you show up every day for your 30 minutes, eventually you will write *something*—a *real* something. Something you can build on, something that is actually moving in the right direction. And by doing this every day, you'll find it will become a habit and, like all habits, it will get easier. You'll get more productive. And then you might even try stealing another 30 minutes so you have a full hour of writing time each day.

It's the same principle as Julia Cameron's morning pages described in her book *The Artist's Way: A Spiritual Path to Higher Creativity.* Whether you write three pages a day or write for 30 minutes a day, adhering to the schedule is a way to train your creativity to surface on demand—a sure way to amass a body of work and keep your writing spirit energized.

Writer Tara Lynne Groth takes a different approach to the time challenge. "Throughout the day I can easily get pulled in a dozen different directions: working on a client project, finding markets to pitch an article, critiquing a story for my group, etc. I might not have time that day to walk my dog or clean the house, but I always make time for meals away from my computer screen," she said.

The connection to her writing? "When I have trouble finding time to write, I turn one of my meals (often breakfast) into a generative writing session. If I only get 10 minutes of writing with my breakfast, and that happens dozens of times throughout the year—that's a lot of hours of writing I would have otherwise missed."

Roadblock #2: Lack of Momentum

There are times when you just can't seem to move forward. Your creative wheels are stuck in the mud and all you're doing is churning up a lot of dirt. You might have fallen into the trap of editing instead of writing. You write three sentences and stop to fix two of them, fiddling with the punctuation or skimming through the thesaurus to find better choices. Or worse, you read your partial draft with a judgmental eye, evaluating its market potential before it's even finished.

But if you start the revision process too early, you could become so intimidated by all the flaws you perceive that you lose your momentum entirely. The solution is simple: train yourself to write first, rewrite second. You need to get your first draft out of your head before you revise it.

Blocked flow can be another problem. It's akin to trying to start an engine that's been sitting idle for far too long. No matter how many times you turn the key, that engine just won't turn over. This is where writing prompts can be useful.

You spend five minutes of your 30-minute writing time doing fun writing activities that have nothing to do with the work at hand. There are loads of books, newsletters and websites where you can find writing prompts, or "jump-starts" as I call them— stress-free ways to warm up your writing engine since it's a "no expectation/no demand" exercise.

When the roadblock seems insurmountable, consider walking away—not permanently, but just long enough to give your Muse a chance to catch his or her breath. Author Kerin Freeman remembered a time when this strategy worked for her.

"I had trouble with one manuscript. I couldn't think of an ending. I spent days mulling it over but nothing seemed to have the impact I was looking for," she recalled. "It eventually came to me in the shower—a Eureka moment, if you will. I find the harder you try, the worse it seems. Your brain just won't collaborate with you. It's better to put your writing away and forget about it for a few weeks or even months. And then, when you dig it out again words, stories, sentences, endings seem to just slot into place."

Roadblock #3: Lack of Stimulation

If you've been following the same routine for some time—writing in the same place at the same time looking at the same four walls— your brain might need a sensory boost. Try doing your 30 minutes in a café, at a museum or even outdoors. Even though you are still focusing on the paper or screen, the change in the environment may have a positive effect on your creativity.

Or before you start your half-hour writing time, get your body moving. An article in *Frontiers in Human Neuroscience,* "The impact of physical exercise on convergent and divergent thinking," cited several studies linking physical exercise and enhanced creative thinking. This was backed up to some extent by the researchers' own work although they did point out that for non-athletes, creativity was actually diminished post-workout. (Yet another reason to avoid couch-potato-itis—it's bad for your writing!)

Other research has shown that physical exercise can enhance the functioning of your prefrontal cortex where your creativity hangs out. So stand up, do some simple stretches or yoga postures, lift weights, go for a walk. This can be especially useful if you're feeling a little dragged out and too pooped to peck at the keys. Just a 15-minute walk in fresh air can work wonders to wake up your mind, get the blood flowing and fill you full of enough energy to complete your half-hour writing work and then some!

And if you're afraid that while you're away from your desk, inspiration will strike, just pack a pen and notepad or use the memo function on your phone to store those brilliant ideas for later retrieval.

Another roadblock buster is to switch your style. If you do most of your writing with the keyboard and computer, write longhand. If you write mostly in silence, experiment with different types of music. In the *Journal of Consumer Research*'s article, "Is Noise Always Bad? Exploring the Effects of Ambient Noise on Creative Cognition," researchers reported that a moderate level of ambient noise (around 70 decibels) can enhance your performance on creative tasks.

Music can also get you in the mood for the type of piece you're working on, whether you choose songs to inspire specific emotions (anger, sorrow, fear) or those that fit the time frame of your story (World War II era songs for stories set in the forties or rock and roll for the sixties).

Editor Paige Duke's article, "How To Always Have Something Awesome To Write About" on the Standout Books website mentions a few other tricks to get things moving, including listening to podcasts, keeping a journal and people-watching—with a dose of eavesdropping to go with it! "One day soon," she wrote encouragingly, "you'll wake to find the muse sitting beside your bed, waiting for you to get to work."

Roadblock #4: Lack of Confidence

Sometimes, all the gods are with us, the muses are lined up on either side of our desk, no one is bothering us—in short, conditions are perfect for writing. And then it starts: our internal gremlins whisper: "You'll never be a writer. Who do you think you are—another Shakespeare? JK Rowling? Stephen King?"

This is the **evil spirit of self-doubt**.

The bad news is that these feelings are part and parcel of being a writer. Even the best writers go through periods of self-doubt and even fear, and that can lead to an inability to write—hence, writer's block. What are some of the fears? Author Wally Wood detailed them: "Fear of failing, or fear of not living up to one's own standards, or fear of not living up to others' expectations, or fear of rejection, or fear of success, or fear of embarrassing your mother, your father, your spouse, your editor."

The good news is that there are some strategies that you can use to help silence those gremlin voices and overcome those fears.

Do a self-analysis of your writing background. Is there a legitimate reason for your lack of confidence? Are you coasting on previous successes or actively increasing your skill level? Are you paying attention to industry changes or just submitting your material to the same old publications?

And how up to date are you on current affairs and topics? This is especially important if you are writing articles because *no* editor wants pitches based on last year's news. If you need to upgrade your skills or knowledge base, there is no time like the present to do it!

Create a Success Résumé. Make a list of the writing work you've done—regardless of whether any of it was published or whether you were paid for it. Magazine articles, short stories, letters to the editor, essays—it doesn't matter *what* you have written but simply *that* you have written. The purpose of this little project is to remind yourself in a very concrete way that you *are* a writer and you have a body of work to prove it.

Beat the self-doubt demons with a little good karma. Remember, *all* writers experience these doubts at one time or another. So, write notes to at least five of your favorite writers telling them how much you love their work, why you love it, and thanking them for sharing their creativity with you. It is entirely possible that your note will reach them when they are doing their own battle with the self-doubt demon and your words will give them just enough ammunition to win out.

Renew your love of writing. Remind yourself of what it is you love about writing by writing about it. Writing is like being in a relationship—when things are going smoothly, we can enumerate all the good points of our beloved, but when we aren't getting along, all we see are the annoying aspects!

When our writing relationship hits a bad patch, we moan about how slow the editors are to accept our articles, how unkind reviewers are about our latest books, or how agents are so unresponsive to our queries. Our complaints can take up hours to list, and the more we complain, the more we hate this writing life we have chosen.

But as author Dawn Reno Langley said, "I do believe we all have the power to get ourselves where we want to be, and that if you put negative energy out into the world, that negative energy will bounce back to you."

Avoid being hit with a negativity boomerang by setting a timer for 15 minutes and write about how much you *love* writing—the act of writing, the outcomes, the people you have met through your writing and the self-realizations that writing has brought to you.

Think back to when you experienced those golden moments—the times when the pen, pencil or keyboard fairly burned with the flame of your creativity or those times when something you wrote connected with a reader, who then took the time to communicate that to you.

This will remind you of why you choose to write and how important the act of writing is to you and will reinvigorate your spirit and build your self-confidence. Then, just sit down and write. Stop looking for reasons why you shouldn't do it, stop listening to all those negative whispers, stop worrying about what other people will think and just write.

No matter where you are in your writing career, roadblocks will occur. But if you can identify the type of obstacle that's in your way, you can develop a strategy for circumventing it so you can get back to what you most want to do: write!

THE PROCRASTINATION PREDICAMENT

"You may delay, but time will not."
Benjamin Franklin

I do a lot of book events and writing workshops, and at each one, without fail, someone will come up to me and say, "I've got a great idea for a book and I'm going to write it someday *as soon as I have the time.*"

I *so* want to tell them that if they are waiting for the Time Fairy to grant them several months, or possibly even years, to produce a manuscript, they'd better settle in for a good long wait. There's no Time Fairy, and there's no guarantee of an open space for writing. All you *have*—all any person *has*—is this moment right now.

"But I don't have time," you protest. "There's work and family and…" and here it comes, the list of reasons why you can't do what you say you want to do. Too often, however, what you believe is a lack of time is really a lack of prioritizing. Think about it. If something is really important to you, you find time for it. You shoehorn it in among all the other items on your To-Do list and, one way or the other, you get it done.

So why not the *writing*? Why have you fallen victim to the Power of Procrastination, that insidious little voice that tells you "There's no rush! You have plenty of time!" instead of moving forward on that project you claim is so near and dear to your heart? What is holding you back?

Very often it is one of the following excuses.

Excuse #1: You're afraid of failing.

Whether this is your first foray into writing or you've completed other pieces but are now trying something new, fear can be a major procrastination-producer. Writing is like being on a tightrope. You can see the end, but between that and the first step stretches a very long, very skinny rope. And that rope doesn't even have the decency to remain still but sways with the winds of change: how you feel, what else is going on in your life, what other people say about your idea.

So you stand there, think about giving it a go, but never really move—too afraid of "falling" (i.e., failing) to take the first step.

What you need to remember is that, when it comes to writing, the only real failure is in *not* writing. All writers—famous or insignificant, published or not—have had work that didn't turn out the way they had hoped. But they didn't allow that to stop them from going back to the desk and trying again.

Thomas Edison said, "If I find 10,000 ways something won't work, I haven't failed. I am not discouraged, because every wrong attempt discarded is often a step forward..." and the same is true of writing. You learn each time you write—about what you do well and where you need to improve, about how to structure your thoughts and when to let your imagination have free rein, about what is your natural talent and what might need some outside assistance through critique groups or workshops.

But this requires you to be open to the learning, to be able to take away from each experience something of value that will allow your next writing project to be better, stronger, richer—more technically and creatively improved over past attempts.

Then start with something easy: a simple task that you know you can complete as recommended by Dr. Jeremy Dean in the PsyBlog article, "10 Foolproof Tips for Overcoming Procrastination." One small success can generate a big boost of encouragement!

Don't know where to begin? Start anywhere, according to the article, to avoid the trap of spending more time *planning* where to start and less time actually *starting*!

Excuse #2: You feel guilty taking time for writing.

Ah, guilt... like Lon Chaney, it's an emotion with a thousand faces: responsibility, self-sacrifice, duty—you name it and guilt is probably behind it. Of *course* you need to fulfill your other obligations, but would spending 30 minutes a day or a few hours a week harm the other people in your life? And if you *were* able to take the time and work on your dream, wouldn't it make you feel better about yourself and your circumstances? And if you *felt* better, wouldn't you be a nicer person to be around?

There is no reason to feel guilty about using the talents you were given and finding new ways to express your thoughts and emotions. The only guilt that should surface is the one that comes when you realize you chose to waste that creative gift.

Excuse #3: It's so big an undertaking that you don't know where to start—so you don't.

You may have a great idea—writing a research-heavy biography of a little-known missionary or starting a freelance writing business—but then you are so overwhelmed by the ramifications of the project you're considering that you can't even start it!

It's not that you don't want to do it—there may be moments when you are really excited about the prospect. But you just can't take those first, all-important steps. To use a trip analogy, your luggage is packed and the gas tank is filled, but you resist starting the engine and heading down the road because you don't know if you have what it takes to complete the journey.

So instead, you *talk* about what you're going to do for weeks or months (or could it even be *years?*), but talking is *all* you have to show for it. You're excited by the idea of it but overwhelmed as well. It's just so darned *big*! Whatever it is, there is something about the project that makes it seem more than you can handle, and so you look for ways to avoid *doing* it and settle for *talking* about doing. And the only way to get out of that talking-not-doing rut is to take the leap.

I "took the leap" in 2016, following my father's death the previous fall. After spending months handling his paperwork and settling his affairs—and not writing—I started feeling the urge to leave my house where he had spent the last few years of his life. Maybe it was a need to distance myself from the grief I was feeling. Maybe it was a need to remind myself that life—*my* life— could still go on.

So I got it into my head to take a 900-mile road trip from Ohio to Florida, justifying the idea as research for a story I was working on about a character who took the same journey. No problem, except that I had never taken a road trip of such an extent on my own and the prospect was exciting—and terrifying. What if the car broke down? What if I became stuck somewhere with no cell phone service? What if I got sick?

As I did all my pre-trip planning—printing out directions, programming the trip into a borrowed GPS and setting the map app on my phone to give me voice directions—this litany of "what ifs" kept playing in my mind until the idea of the trip became something to be feared, not anticipated. But by this time, I had already scheduled some book signings and workshops, so I couldn't back out.

So I forced myself to stop thinking about the big picture and, every day, concentrated on doing just one thing. I arranged for someone to take care of the house. I bought non-perishables to munch on the way. I pulled my summer clothes out of storage since Florida would be considerably warmer in April than northeast Ohio!

And finally, on the day of my departure, I pulled out of my driveway and didn't look back. And each time the extent of the journey—900 miles!—threatened to overwhelm me, I broke it down to just two hours: in two hours I would stop and take a break. And then I would drive for another two hours. And then stop again.

Reducing the trip to incremental mini-journeys from one two-hour destination to another made it feel more doable. And that's how I made it from Youngstown to St. Augustine—by linking together a series of two-hour drives.

You can use the same idea to overcome your "overwhelmed-itis" issue. Just pick one small task and start working on it. Tell yourself that you'll spend a half hour or so taking a little writing "journey": draft some dialogue or outline the top-line plot points, research markets for your article or clients for your copywriting service. You aren't trying to do everything—the book, the article, the business—all at once. You're just completing one leg of your trek.

The next time, you "drive" a little farther toward your destination. Eventually, as you get deeper into the project, you spend longer periods of time and work on larger chunks until one day you realize your goal is in sight.

That's the same strategy used by Catherine Wald, author of *The Resilient Writer: Tales of Rejection and Triumph by 23 Top Authors*. As she freely admitted, "I am the world's greatest procrastinator. I'll even do things I hate to do instead of what I need to do. When my kids were young and I was working part-time, I told my husband, 'If you ever come home and the house is spotlessly clean, you'll know I didn't get any of my work done.'"

What can make her fall victim to the "delay-and-defer disease"? "When I feel overwhelmed with the magnitude of everything I have to do. Much to my dismay, I can't sit down at my desk in the morning and organize my entire life. However, I can make a to-do list and at least cross some of the items out," she said, adding, "It really does help to break a project down in teeny tiny segments and take them one at a time. Instead of failing at a big task, you can succeed at numerous small tasks and still be moving toward your goal."

It doesn't matter if your goal is to save $100,000 or write 100,000 words. Doing it dollar by dollar, or in this case, paragraph by paragraph, will inevitably help you reach your goal.

Excuse #4: Your motivation is less than optimal.

There are projects that you can't wait to work on, that you think about all day long and dream about at night. Projects that thrill you, excite you and fill you with joy. And then, there are the other projects—the ones that you have to do because you have agreed to it or because it is a necessary part of a bigger objective. When those crop up on your To-Do list, the temptation to ignore them can be almost irresistible. The problem is, like a splinter in your finger, they can cause a level of psychic discomfort that can affect your overall productivity.

Paige Duke said she often faces the procrastination problem in her editing work. While she sets a daily quota for each project in order to meet her final deadlines, she admitted that "with less exciting subject matter, I do sometimes just have the thought: 'Ugh, I don't want to do this.' When that happens, I am tempted to procrastinate or save it until last; but, of course, that will backfire and put me behind schedule."

Her strategy? "I work in a 'fun' space, like a coffee shop or outside in my backyard if the weather is nice, or have a treat, either alongside the work or as a reward for finishing it—for me that's a cup of coffee or a fun snack!" Duke's other tricks are tackling the work when she has the most energy and breaking the daily quota into even smaller pieces. "I work on it in between my other projects or tasks for that day," she explained. "This just makes it more bearable."

Excuse #5: You're not sure if you really want to write.

In her book, *Write Away*, author Elizabeth George noted that many people don't necessarily want to do all the hard work associated with producing a quality piece of writing. They simply "want to have written"—have that byline or see their name on the book cover.

While you may like the idea of *having* your work published, the hours spent actually *doing* the work doesn't exactly appeal to you. You want instant completion, followed by instant acceptance, publication and fame. Don't we all! But the reality of writing is that no one knows for certain what the outcome will be.

Instead, each writer—by which I mean, each *real* writer—approaches the new project with a mix of excitement and trepidation. Excitement because to bring a new idea to life and give it a fixed tangible form generates a heady sense of power. Trepidation because every writer has had the experience of getting a few paragraphs, pages or even chapters completed and then realizing that it's going nowhere, that the idea that seemed so viable the day before now could be headed for life support or the plot that appeared so clear cut has now become impossibly convoluted.

For every completed work, there are probably a hundred false starts. But that's okay, too. It's just the way the process goes. But if you are the type of person who can't handle setbacks and rejection, then your issue is not really procrastination but something more basic and ultimately insurmountable: you just don't want to *do* the work to get to where you *say* you want to go.

And in that case, no amount of time is going to solve your problem.

This is where you need to do some serious self-examination. Why do you want to write? Why do you want to be a writer? When you think about what it means to you, what do you envision: the fame and fortune that you're certain writing will bring to you or the pleasure that you associate with doing the work? (Not that there is anything wrong with fame *or* fortune, but since there is no guarantee you'll get either or both, you'd better have some *other* reason to sustain you during those long hours that precede the outcome!)

How committed are you to your writing dream—enough to put in the time and effort, to accept the sacrifices you need to make, to give up something else to make this dream turn into reality? And make no mistake about it, whatever your dream is— write a book or become a full-time freelancer—it will cost something in terms of time, money and effort. But then, anything worth having comes at a price. Only you know if you are ready to pay it.

How do you know if your tendency to procrastinate is really a problem that you need to deal with? According to an article about procrastination on The Writing Center at UNC-Chapel Hill website, it's when *not* doing something or avoiding a task ultimately makes you feel discouraged or overburdened. Essentially, while procrastination may work in the short term, over time, the effect can become more and more uncomfortable.

Think of it like a pebble in your shoe. You might be able to walk a block or two despite the irritation, but eventually you'll have to do one of two things: deal with the stone or stop walking. If, in this case, you've decided to deal with the procrastination "pebble," then you need to take actionable steps.

Some of the tips listed in The Writing Center's article include creating a productive environment, asking for help and making yourself accountable. The last can be especially useful if you involve another person in your plan, someone whom you check in with on a set schedule to share your progress. (Hint: don't choose another procrastinator!)

This is where having a Writing Success Team—people with whom you can stay in touch virtually or in person—can be extremely helpful.

The Value of a Writing Success Team

Members of a Writing Success Team fall into one of three categories:

- The Encouragers

- The Challengers

- The Expert Sources

Encouragers are the people who keep your spirit up, the cheer-leaders of your team. These are the ones you call when you've just received your tenth rejection and need someone to tell you that you don't stink as a writer! They aren't necessarily involved in the industry but are people who wish the best for you and want to see you succeed.

Challengers are the people who won't let you make excuses or get away with all the rationalizations you offer for *not* writing but instead act as "cattle prods" or coaches pushing you to keep going. They also challenge your negative thinking (e.g., "No one ever gets published without knowing someone!"), forcing you to justify your rationale.

Their role is less about making you feel *good* and more about making sure you don't fall into the habit of viewing every setback as an example of Fate's being against you or the general unfairness of the writing world. They also know your tendencies and bad habits—perhaps better than you might like!—and will point out any evidence that you are letting them get in your way.

Finally, Expert Sources are the people who are knowledgeable about the writing profession, the fact-based people, the teachers who educate you about the art and business of writing. They can range from workshop leaders to other writers and authors. They are industry professionals: those who have been in the writing business in one way or another and have extensive information available to share.

Attending a workshop or seminar is one way to connect with an expert source. I have also found some of my best "expert sources" at author events where, for example, millennial authors give me advice on social media marketing and building a street team while self-published authors share their tips for doing it right the first time.

You don't even necessarily have to meet your Expert Source face-to-face. You can gain valuable insights into how to develop as a writer and writing professional by signing up for a webinar and reading books or newsletters from recognized authorities in the business.

Ideally, as you develop your Writing Success Team, you'll have at least one person in each category. That way your team will be balanced, and you'll get the right kind of support to help you grow and develop as a writer and beat your procrastination proclivity!

CREATING YOUR WRITING SPACE

"...a woman must have money and a room of her own if she is to write fiction" Virginia Woolf

While Woolf was focusing on the requirements for women writing fiction, the fact is, regardless of the type of writing you do or what your sex is, having a place devoted exclusively to your writing can make all the difference in the world, not only in terms of your output but also in how you *feel* about your craft.

A specific area for writing not only gives the act importance and identifies it as something of value but also requires a commitment from you. If you have managed to carve out a few square feet or, if you're lucky, an entire room for your creative endeavor, then you darned well better use it!

The point is that if you are dedicated to pursuing your craft, you should also have a dedicated space for doing it, even if, at the end of your writing time, it changes from being your expansive writing desk back to the table where everyone gathers for dinner.

So let's talk about what constitutes a writing space for you, including your must-haves and must-nots. How large does it have to be and what items have earned the right to inhabit it? And where exactly is the writing space located—in your home or somewhere else?

The Must-Haves and Must-Nots

There is no one "right" working space for a writer as the images shown in Booktique's "The Writing Space of famous writers" and BuzzFeed's "40 Inspiring Workspaces Of The Famously Creative" illustrate. What do you *need* in your writing room? A good light, a flat surface and a comfortable yet supportive chair are all givens.

If your space is doing double-duty—writing room by day, family room by night—choose pieces that fall in the "resimercial" category, as explained by Blake Zalcberg, president of OFM (an office and school furniture manufacturer and distributor).

"Instead of traditional workplace white or black, it often comes in muted colors like blues and grays that match furniture styles and colors people already have in their homes," he said. "The furniture is designed to blend in seamlessly with the rest of the house, so that there is less of a dividing line between your home office and home."

Once you have the basics, the other accoutrements are up to you. Some writers select accessories and images that are in some way connected to the project at hand while others prefer those that more broadly inspire their creativity. The idea is to select those items that, in some way, reference your writing life or reinforce your identity as a writer.

In her "Creation Station," children's author Cat Michael has a collection of playthings, quilted wall hangings she made herself, a 6-inch rubber version of Rodin's "The Kiss" and framed prints from art exhibits and photos taken by her great-grandfathers. She also has "a few well-behaved plants that don't mind neglect or my talking to them."

Across from my desk, I have shadow boxes holding copies of my books and the anthologies to which I have contributed. These represent goals I have achieved. To my right are three bookshelves, full of the output of other authors, serving as support and encouragement. "You're not alone," those books seem to say. "You can do it. We did."

Finally, behind me, I have what I call my "Power Board": a large bulletin board with postcards, images and quotations that in some way link to my writing identity or goals. Why *behind* me? Because I can feel the push of those elements propelling me forward.

Before I sit down at my desk, I glance at what's posted there: the encouraging note from my friend, author and playwright Morrow Wilson, magazine pictures of various "dream office" spaces and all the other bits and pieces that I have pinned to the board.

My favorite? An image featuring a sleeping polar bear with a penguin standing on his back, holding a pair of cymbals, while above the two is the caption "Do one brave thing today... then run like hell!"

While over the months and years you may have filled your space with bits and pieces that worked for you, maybe lately it seems they haven't been doing their job. Or it might be that your writing dream has changed and these no longer fit your new creative path.

If your inspiration needs a bit of a boost, maybe it's time to practice some writer-focused feng shui or space clearing. Change out the items on your desk and get rid of the clutter. Just because you always had the same pictures and tchotchkes in your workspace for the past several years doesn't mean you can't switch them out for something new or, at the very least, move them to another location!

When I had a more confined space, my file cabinets were scattered throughout the house: some upstairs and others in the basement. Once I moved into my current 440-square-foot office, I had to decide what files should be part of the space. The only client materials brought into the office were those connected to current projects, so I had more room to allocate to my short stories, essays and books in progress. By giving more physical space to my own writing, I was also giving it more psychic space as well, thereby underlining its priority in my writing life.

Evaluate and examine every item that you bring into your writing "home," only keeping those that, in one fashion or another, serve to inspire your creativity. And don't overlook the effect that color can play in your writing space.

According to Pantone's "What are the characteristics of color?" article, cool colors (blues to violets) can have a calming effect while warm colors (reds to yellows) are active, attention-grabbing and aggressive.

"There are colors that we can say almost everyone has the same response to," noted principal designer Lisa Peck, ASID, of Minneapolis-based LiLu Interiors. "For example, purple can inspire a sense of calmness and creativity, while yellow can promote optimism, wisdom and introspection and innovation."

Equally important, she added, is to have a balance in the hues you bring into your room.

"While purple inspires creativity, it doesn't really help you be gregarious or extroverted, which might be the feeling you need for the type of piece you're working on. Bringing in some orange can help you express what you're trying to say. Adding a complementary color—one across the color wheel from the shade you have in your space—can also make a room feel more active and create an energetic vibration."

Keep in mind, however, that the hues that once revved up your writing engine might not be doing the trick. That's when it's important to shake things up, said California-based artist, author, architectural color expert and interior designer Cristina Acosta.

"If you're stuck, it wouldn't hurt to change your space, regardless of the color. Go toward what you hate. Go toward what you love. You have to find a way to continually change and challenge your environment so it keeps you fresh."

Acosta said to determine what your writing "nest" needs to look like "and how it needs to serve you, and also when it's time to leave it and find or build a new one." And if you can't physically leave the "nest," making dramatic changes in the color can make you feel like you've entered into a new and more energized one. Not up to changing the color in the entire room? Maybe an accent wall will do the trick!

As for those small or dark spaces (think the "writer's garret" or the reverse: the "writer's basement"), color can help offset structural negatives. To maximize light, choose a semi-gloss to high-gloss paint finish so the light reflects off the wall, said Acosta.

Mirrors and paintings can do double duty: they not only add visual interest to the room but also give your eye somewhere to focus other than on the screen or paper in front of you, thus helping to reduce eye fatigue.

Another trick is to use a monochromatic color scheme to make the room appear larger and feel more open, said Peck. A mix of lighting can also help, especially for those spaces without a good source of natural light.

"You want good general lighting but it doesn't have to be super bright throughout the room," Peck said. "Overhead lighting should be softer and warmer, like that produced by incandescent bulbs which fall in the 2700 range on the Kelvin scale, while task lighting right at where you're working should be brighter and more focused. Having that difference in the light levels can also help the room feel larger."

Not sure what light to choose? The Westinghouse site (www.westinghouselighting.com/color-temperature.aspx) has a great article on creating ambiance with light.

123 Writer Lane

Choosing the ideal locale for your creative "home" can be challenging. Not everyone has a spare room to turn into an office. According to her autobiography, even prolific author Agatha Christie didn't have a "room of her own" until more than a decade after she published her first book, *The Mysterious Affair at Styles*.

Many writers have to make do with what space is available to them. For example, writer and editor Ann Henry and her husband live on a 50-foot sailboat. She does her work in the dinette where the table and settees provide her with space to spread out her materials. The drawback, she noted, is that "when we are under way, I can't really use the computer, so I just write by hand in a notebook."

Author Sandra Gurvis's "writing room" has changed over the years, from being in the basement of her house or a cubbyhole the size of a broom closet to a spare bedroom. But wherever it's located, she said, "I make it look like an office with desk, chairs, files, and the best computer equipment I can afford."

Author Charles Weinblatt works on his books in the family room overlooking a densely-wooded ravine inhabited by "all kinds of beautiful flora and fauna. With a very popular bird feeder just outside a window, it's like living in a zoo."

For years, writer Barb Routen's workspace was in a corner of a common room in her house, "which wasn't conducive to uninterrupted work," she noted. "When one of our sons left home, I appropriated his bedroom. I painted it, replaced the decades-old carpet with shiny wood and put an Oriental-style area rug under my desk chair. I hung inspiring paintings, quotes and framed awards I've received on the walls. The room is away from the most-active parts of the house, providing me privacy for phone interviewing and concentration when I'm involved in planning or writing a story."

And in the spirit of "if you can't beat 'em, join 'em!", novelist and father-of-two Scott Southard writes "on the fly and when I can. That can be at a table, on my iPhone (I've written entire blogposts on my iPhone), or anywhere with a flat surface. It all comes down to inspiration and the accessibility around it. On a good weekend, I like to go to a coffee shop on Sunday for a few hours; sadly, I haven't had a chance to do that in a while. I assume the coffee shop has my table roped off for me still."

These days, I do my writing on a spacious L-shaped desk. But in the past, I have written on a much smaller table in a cold and unfinished area of my basement, on a tray table at my parents' California condo, and (the most uncomfortable space to date) in a hotel bathroom perched on the toilet lid with my laptop on my lap, the only place with an accessible working outlet. (I do not recommend it, and yes, I did get a room discount when I checked out the next morning!)

And while I like to be alone when I write, that has not always been an option. Crowded gate areas at airports and hospital rooms are among the shared spaces where I have had to "ply my craft" when my writing schedule and life or travel plans collided.

Mobile Writing Spaces

For many writers, working at home can be the ideal situation. It's convenient, saves gas (no commuting required) and is relatively immune to the impact of the inclement weather. (Although losing power due to snowstorms or lightning strikes can slow the process down a bit!)

Others find the domestic environment too distracting (think kids, spouse, household chores) or lacking in available workable space, so they choose to work elsewhere. That was the challenge faced by middle-grade and young-adult author Rod Martinez. A recent move meant he lost his "creative room" as he called it, so these days he does his writing at the library, bookstores and cafés or, for absolute silence, "in bed, on my laptop late at night while everyone else sleeps."

Other suggestions for off-site writing spaces are conservatories, museums, parks or botanical gardens as well as local libraries—a haven for your writing brain.

"Libraries are a writer's dream," said Laurie Kincer, Writers' Center Specialist at the William N. Skirball Writers' Center at the South Euclid-Lyndhurst Branch of the Cuyahoga County Public Library in Ohio. "They offer information and inspiration: books and magazines on writing, special subscriptions to self-publishing tools such as SELF-e and Pressbooks, library databases for general or historical research, and trained reference librarians to assist. They also supply the quiet space you need to write. And where else can you spend the entire day, with access to a world of information, without having to pay anything or buy anything?"

The South Euclid Writers' Center is just one example of how libraries are adapting to the needs of area writers. It's a writer's ideal space: two rooms available for private writing time or group sessions, a large open area with tables and chairs, small couches and a booth space for writing as well as a fireplace and a wall of windows. It's the first dedicated, staffed writers' center at an Ohio public library, said Kincer, who credited the vision of library director Sari Feldman for its creation.

The Center for Fiction at the Mercantile Library in New York City is the only organization in the United States devoted solely to the vital art of fiction. Its sky-lit space is available to writers of all genres and people at all different stages of their career, with desks, a lounge area and a kitchenette/refreshment room stocked with the essentials: coffee, water and candy!

The four Writer's Rooms at the Nashville Public Library in Nashville, Tennessee can be used for up to six months although they are restricted to those meeting specific requirements, such as a signed publisher's contract or publisher's letter of interest, visiting scholars and academicians, and authors and journalists. And at the Multnomah County Library's Sterling Room for Writers in Portland, Oregon, writers can work on their projects in a dedicated space with convenient access to library holdings.

Need to get even farther away from your home? The Artist-in-Residence (AIR) programs available through the National Park Service might be just the ticket. According to the website, most residencies are two to four weeks in length and are available for visual artists, writers, musicians, and those working in other creative media.

These are just a few of the locations available for writers. Chances are, there is bound to be a perfect writing home-away-from-home somewhere close to you!

While working in a library pretty much guarantees a degree of quiet, other places could prove sound-challenging. If you need to block out noise from those in close proximity, try wearing ear-plugs or headphones. Working at home but not alone? Invest in a white noise machine, also known as a sound conditioner, to mask the clamor.

Or, if total silence is too deafening, download white-noise apps, ranging from natural sounds (waves crashing on a beach or the blowing of the wind) to man-made ones: airplane travel or the clothes dryer. The myNoise.net, a website run by Stéphane Pigeon, PhD, has a wide range of sounds, including natural, industrial, tonal drones and atmosphere to play on your computer or via mobile app. Feeling isolated? Try "Café Restaurant," a coffee-shop background noise generator, to have the illusion that you are not alone!

"Such noises are more effective than one thinks at first glance," said Pigeon. He recommended that writers "keep working with these noises in the background. If you are actively listening to them, it won't work. The goal is to have your brain forget about them and create the illusion of silence round you. These noises have been optimized to cover a wide frequency range, and block audible distractions around you. By reducing the distractions, you increase focus and reduce procrastination."

There are also some tricks for turning a public location into your private writing space. A tip from Acosta is to have a specific article of clothing or outfit that represents your "writing clothes": when you wear them, you are in your "writing room," even if you are really in a crowded restaurant.

You can also pack a few little items—for instance, a mug you only use when you're writing—to create your private writing space. Going back to color, Acosta recommended bringing "a placemat or swatch of material in a shade that makes you feel creative and lay it across the table to create a boundary and a place. It's a demarcation and also part of the writing ritual: 'This is my work time.'"

In the end, whether you work at home or away, you need to create a writing "room of your own" to encourage your creativity to flourish.

YOUR WRITING TOOLBOX

"There is always, of course, that terrible three weeks, or a month, which you have to get through when you are trying to get started on a book. There is no agony like it..." Agatha Christie (from Agatha Christie: An Autobiography)

In one corner of my basement is my workroom. That's where I have a six-foot-tall tool chest, a workbench and a shelving unit holding three parts cabinets with drawers filled with nuts, bolts, screws and nails, hinges and light chains, mirror brackets and... well, you get the picture.

If something breaks, there's a very good chance that *somewhere* in my little storehouse of stuff, I have *something* that I can use to fix it.

What does that have to do with writing? If you have a good collection of "tools," then when your writing process breaks down, you can head over there to find something that will get it working again.

What should you store in your writing toolbox? What strategies can help inspire you? Here are suggestions to try—some physical, some psychological.

Establish a Writing Routine

You might be in your writing place *physically*, but are you there psychologically? One of the best ways of getting yourself into the writing groove is to establish a regular routine for the process. Clear off your desk so your muse has a place to perch, then do some simple stretches to get the blood moving for the work ahead. (Don't think writing is work? Just ask the rest of us who have carpal tunnel syndrome, sore neck muscles or a stiff upper back from too many hours spent hunched over the keyboard!)

Use your journal to explore your thoughts on writing in general or, more specifically, on the current project—a great place to vent if things aren't going as smoothly as you'd like! Or use it to do your "morning pages"—three pages of stream-of-consciousness writing popularized by Julia Cameron in *The Artist's Way*.

Light a candle or use a diffuser to infuse your space with the writing "fragrance" that suits your need. In "6 Scents That Can Transform Your Mood and Productivity" on the Entrepreneur.com website, health and lifestyle freelance journalist Lisa Evans recommended lemon and cinnamon to promote concentration, while lavender can help ease emotional stress caused by that dreaded combination of a looming deadline and writer's block.

In "Aromatherapy Scents to Increase Productivity" on the Productivity Theory website, writer Kayla Matthews suggested jasmine to generate a touch of euphoria or peppermint or eucalyptus to help you brainstorm. And in her article "7 Scents That Boost Productivity And Help You Focus—Even When You're Exhausted" on Rodale's Organic Life website, writer Allison Young noted that the smell of coffee can help counter the mid-afternoon slump and suggested keeping a jar of coffee beans on your desk for a quick caffeine-fix inhale.

Say a prayer to those saints or gods or goddesses associated with the arts. The Roman Catholic saints Cecilia and Columba are the patrons of poets while St. Francis de Sales and the Archangel Gabriel cover journalists. (Not surprisingly given his role in delivering messages from on high, Gabriel is more broadly the patron saint of communication!)

Or reach out to the ancient gods and goddesses. Athena is the Greek goddess of wisdom while Bragi is the Norse god of poetry and eloquence. In Armenian mythology, Tir is the god of written language, sharing the role with the Egyptian goddess Seshat, also credited with inventing writing *and* the alphabet.

Meditation is another way to center your mind and block out all those distractions (household chores, bills, rejection letters) that can affect your ability to focus on the work at hand. Author Dianne Schwartz is a firm believer in the meditative practice, having used it successfully when she was writing her first book.

"As writers, we are accustomed to researching and asking questions of others for a project but sometimes, we also need to listen, and that's what meditation is—listening. When I was writing my book, *Whose Face Is in the Mirror?*, I would lie on the floor, close my eyes and basically study the back of my eyelids. Wonderful colors would float by and as I relaxed more deeply, words came to my mind and soon, the more I did this, entire chapters were written in my thoughts. My meditation practice led to inspiration and Divine Assistance." She added, "Meditation will not only make you a better writer but can lead to a spirituality beginning to evolve that is life-changing."

At the start of a new project, author and poet Fran Orenstein uses a whiteboard to "list location, characters, their bios and a brief story-line. Then I'm psyched to start chapter one," she explained, adding, "If I am growing bored with or unsure about a novel in progress, I go back and reread it or at least the last part written, to get myself psyched again. I call it editing as a jump-start."

While some writers need absolute silence, relying on closed doors, white-noise machines or headphones to block out the rest of the world, others may prefer some background sounds, somewhere in the 70-decibel range. In "Turn It Up: How the Right Amount of Ambient Noise Increases Creativity" on 99u.

com, writer Dave Burkus cited research done by Ravi Mehta, Rui (Juliet) Zhu and Amar Cheema.

"Background noise creates a distraction, but balance is key," Burkus wrote. "A moderate level of background noise creates just enough distraction to break people out of their patterns of thinking and nudge them to let their imagination wander, while still keeping them from losing their focus on the project"—a sensory balancing act that can enhance your creativity.

Stéphane Pigeon, PhD, who runs the myNoise.net website, pointed out that sound is a great source of inspiration. "It can trigger emotions, and these emotions will further inspire you. I have many writers in my user community. Many of them are fantastic novelists, enjoying the inspiration created by my darker soundscapes. Using a soundscape that relates to the scene you are writing (e.g. playing thunder in the background when writing a scene that happens in the rain) can also help."

You can also assemble a playlist of your favorite songs or artists, either for general inspiration or specific to the work at hand. After all, you probably have a playlist for your workouts. Why not have one for writing? That's what best-selling romance author Roni Loren does. Loren said that music can serve to set the mood for a scene she is working on or even inspire an entire story, and on her website, she shares the playlists associated with her books.

"Music has always played a role in my writing," said Loren. "The first romance I wrote, *Wanderlust*, was about a rockstar, so it was natural to find inspirational songs while I was writing that one. But then as I moved forward in my career, I realized that each book has its own personality and some songs just speak to the story in a perfect way. Sometimes a song might inspire an idea in a book, but it also works in reverse. Sometimes while I'm writing a book, I hear a song and I'm struck with how well it fits the story. Either way, I feel that music adds another layer to my writing process. So making soundtracks for the books and having playlists like 'Writing Caffeine' (which gets me pumped up to write) or 'The Sexy Stuff' (which can help with writing love scenes) definitely helps me get words onto the page. Plus, readers love the soundtracks too, so that's an added bonus."

Some of my favorite collections are Spencer Brewer's *Where Angels Dance* and Suzanne Ciani's *Pianissimo* and *Pianissimo II*. I also have a playlist that features Carly Simon's "It Happens Every Day," Tina Turner's "Till the Right Man Comes Along" and, of course, Carrie Underwood's "Before He Cheats" that I use when I'm working on one of my novels—perfect selections since the main character was dumped by her long-time lover.

Collect Some Writing Flotsam and Jetsam

Let's start with some physical items. For example, over the years, I have amassed a collection of keys—car keys, door keys, safe keys, suitcase keys, keys that I have no idea what they belong to but are old and interesting in appearance.

Sometimes, when I'm looking for inspiration for a piece of fiction, I'll pull out my key box and randomly pick a key out of the mix and write about it. What does it lock—or unlock? Who owned the key and is that person still searching for it? If I found the door the key will open, what or who will be on the other side?

Natural objects like seashells or unusual rocks, man-made items like mugs or old tin cans, flea market finds like a baby's silver spoon, a wallet or a piece of jewelry can all provide you with a trigger for your imagination. For example, when writer Tara Lynne Groth organizes generative workshops, she uses "prompts that I don't see used in traditional workshops: essential oils to spur memories with aromas, century-old postcards found in thrift shops, old photographs, color swatches, found objects, etc."

There's no limit to what your imagination can make of the most common, everyday item. Having an assortment of odds and ends is like creating a literary bank account: "money" (in the form of creativity triggers) is there ready for withdrawal.

Assemble Your Personal Image Gallery

Besides keys, I also like to save pictures from newspapers and magazines—some that accompanied articles while others were graphics for ads—that, for whatever reason, caught my eye. When I am looking for something to grease my writing gears, I'll pull out the folder, extract one at random, and just start writing about it: what I think the story is about, how it makes me feel, who is in the picture.

Visit an art gallery and view the portraits and then write about one of the subjects depicted in a painting: What is he or she doing? What emotion does the person's expression project—and what event could have generated that reaction? If there is more than one person in the painting, imagine their relationship to each other and write a few lines of dialogue that might take place before or after the sitting.

Or think about the artist: Why did he or she choose that subject? What is the nature of *their* relationship? And what will happen after the artist puts down the brush?

No images handy? Then visit a royalty-free image site online. You can start with a word and see what images it generates or just pick an image out of the selection already on display. Using that visual, start writing. You might only get as far as a couple hundred words or so before putting it aside. Other times, you may end up writing a complete piece. But regardless of the result, it serves as a good creativity exercise because there is no expectation or pressure attached to the outcome.

Take a Book Trek

Go to a bookstore, but rather than going right to your favorite genre, traverse the sections that are not among those you usually visit. Your purpose is not necessarily to select a book to take home with you (not that doing so is *ever* a bad idea!) but simply to look at the titles. Don't examine the inside or back cover copy to learn what the book is about, but instead imagine what the story *could* be. Let your mind wander down the side road of "what if?" and envision the possibilities that could result from a story of the same name.

This works regardless of the type of writing you do. For instance, a detective novel entitled *Mystery at Hollow Creek* could just as easily be a nonfiction story about pollution, a medical drama about a rash of illnesses or a ghost story.

Alternatively, you can use the cover image as an inspiration jump-start. What does the picture make you think of: a person, place, event? Where does your mind go when you look at the colors or the typography? How do you feel when you see the words or the images? While your mind is still exploring the connections, draft some ideas or even the beginning of a piece.

Do the "Limbic Limbo"

Color can do more than perk up your writing area. It can also take you back in time, acting as a kind of visual memory, which can be particularly useful if you are working on a memoir or drawing on your personal history for a piece of fiction.

As principal designer Lisa Peck, ASID, of Minneapolis-based LiLu Interiors explained, "People are drawing on their own experiences when they are writing. So if you are hitting a bump, think about a color that you associate with that time in your life and add a bit of that to your writing space: a piece of art or framed fabric or even a mosaic made from paint chips."

It's the idea of triggering a "color memory"—specific shades that can generate an emotional reaction—that you are going for, she said. "That memory that you associate with that color can help you dip into those past experiences," not unlike the emotions you feel when you hear a song that reminds you of a time in your life, she explained. "Color can have that same kind of association, and you'll find that you respond differently to those colors than other people might."

Scents or aromas can also serve as triggers because your sense of smell is part of the limbic system, the part of the brain involved with emotions, memory formation and motivations. Certain aromas or fragrances can take you back in time, noted writer Christopher Bergland in "How Does Scent Drive Human Behavior?" in *Psychology Today*.

"Researchers call this 'Proustian memory effect,'" he wrote, adding, "Childhood memories linked to scent stay with people throughout life." (For more on this, read *The Proust Effect: The Senses as Doorways to Lost Memories* by Dutch author and scientific researcher Cretien van Campen.)

Whenever I open a fresh can of ground coffee, I am transported back to my grandmother's kitchen where she brewed coffee in an old-fashioned stovetop percolator. Is there a smell that takes you back into the past: your father's after-shave lotion, your uncle's pipe tobacco, the baby powder scent you forever associate with the last child born in your family? The smell of crayons or modeling clay or cinnamon? Any of those can stimulate your memory and, from there, inspire a story, an essay or an article.

Fish in the Word Pond

Two other useful items for your toolbox are sitting on your bookshelf: a dictionary and a thesaurus. Start with the dictionary. Open to any page, pick out a word and start writing, using that word as the jump-start. Or make a list of 10 words from various pages and use them in a short (300 or so-word) piece: poetry, fiction or nonfiction.

Use your thesaurus: pick a paragraph from something you're working on and research other word choices. Or do it in reverse: pick a word from the thesaurus and use it to spark a few lines or short descriptive paragraph. (Don't have the physical books? There are online resources as well!)

And while we're talking reference materials, pick up a few books of writing prompts. Every day choose one to warm up your writing engine. *The 3 A.M. Epiphany* and *The 4 A.M. Breakthrough* (both by Brian Kiteley) and *The Writer's Idea Book* by Jack Heffron are great options as is the *500 Writing Prompts* by Piccadilly Books—a combination writing prompt and journal.

You can also sign up to receive a daily writing prompt to get you started. Search online for "writing prompts" and you'll find more than enough to inspire you.

Try a Kick-Starter

For a change of pace, begin your writing session with some "kick-starters." Start with a line or two of dialogue and keep going from there. (This is where the ability to eavesdrop and remember what you overheard can come in very handy!)

Here are a few examples I have used in my workshops:

1. "Are you kidding me?"

2. "Before I leave, I have one more thing to say."

3. "First, you'll need a large, very sharp knife. Myself, I prefer a cleaver."

4. "I found it on the beach under a piece of driftwood."

5. "I told you I would be there."

6. "It's always later than you think."

7. "It's free. Really. Try it."

8. "It's okay. It doesn't matter. Don't worry about it."

9. "Open the drawer. Take the gun. Close the drawer."

10. "So what do I do now?"

11. "To the best of my recollection, he wasn't part of the group."

12. "What were you thinking?"

13. "Where did you go?"

14. "Where's Billy? I thought he was with you!"

15. "Yes. Absolutely. No problem. I'd love to."

You can also create new endings for familiar aphorisms, such as:

- _____ makes the world go 'round.

- A stitch in time _____

- A bird in the hand _____

- A friend in need _____

- To err is human, to forgive is _____

- When life hands you a lemon _____

- The squeaky wheel _____

- Idle hands are _____

- A penny saved _____

- You can lead a horse to water but _____

- The shortest distance between two points is _____

- An apple a day _____

Go for A Writing Switcheroo

Another useful "tool" is to write in a completely different form from the one you normally use. For example, most of my creative writing is fiction, with an occasional foray into essays. So for me to try my hand at poetry, either rhyming or free verse, would be a major creative stretch. But that's the point: to stretch beyond what you usually do and try something different.

Explore a new genre or a new type of writing. The worst that can happen is that you realize that, at this stage in your writing life, it's not your strongest skill. (Notice I said "at this stage"—you may find in a few years that your interest and ability in that particular writing format has developed!)

Accept a Writing Challenge

You can also undertake writing challenges, such as doing a six-word story, inspired by this one supposedly written by Hemingway: "For sale. Baby shoes. Never worn." (For the record, Hemingway's connection to this has never been definitively established.)

Another version of the six-word story is to write your own life story in six words. Or write a 26-sentence story, starting each sentence with a different letter of the alphabet—in order.

Don't like numbers? Here's a fun prompt: write a love letter instead. Only not to your nearest and dearest but rather to your most beloved, most essential, can't-live-without-it household appliance or office item. It's a great exercise to do in a writing group, especially if the item to whom the letter is addressed is never identified. When the letters are read aloud, the rest of the group has to guess what is the object of the writer's affection.

Take a Crack at Clichés

Ah, those pesky little clichés. They show up in our work, sneaking in when our backs are turned, and all too often manage to go unnoticed. This writing exercise not only lists some common ones but gives you a chance to come up with alternatives for the bracketed sections!

- As plain as [the nose on your face]

- As slow as [molasses]

- Black as [night]

- Blind as [a bat]

- Cold as [death]

- Fresh as [a daisy]

- Give them an inch, and [they'll take a mile]

- Quiet as [a church mouse]

- Smart as [a whip]

- Smooth as [silk]

- White as [snow]

Engage in Future Thinking

This is a dual-purpose writing exercise. Imagine that you've finished the project that is so dear to your heart—your novel, your collection of poetry, the history of a famous event. Now you have to promote it *and* yourself. Write your biography, not as the person you are now, but as the writer who has achieved something to brag about. What do you want to tell the world about your writing process, your inspiration, your next project?

Why is it dual-purpose? First, you have to imagine yourself as someone you aren't—at least, not yet. And by writing about a future event, you might be more motivated to make it come true!

Reflect, Remember, then Write

Your memory is a wellspring of inspiration that you can call upon. One exercise involves recalling someone that you know well, a person you have spent enough time with to be able to recall certain details.

Make a list of everything you can remember, from that person's idiosyncrasies to his or her familiar words or gestures, food preferences or music dislikes. Was there something that person did that irritated you or, conversely, some unique action that, every time you saw it, filled you with love? Be as precise and specific as possible. This is an excellent practice to enhance your skill at creating realistic fictional characters.

Another option is to go back to your childhood. What did you do on a hot, humid summer afternoon or on a winter day that was so cold your eyelashes froze? What toys did you have, what games did you play? What did you eat and drink, what smells, tastes, sights and sounds are part of your childhood?

One of the best parts about using writing prompts is that they are recyclable. You can use the same prompt more than once, but each time you do, you are bringing something new to the table, and so your response to that prompt changes.

Remember, regardless of what strategy, tip or technique you use, the important part is to keep writing—and keep adding more "tools" to your writing toolbox!

LIVING THE WRITING LIFE

"Happy is the heart [of] him who writes; he is young each day..." Papyrus Lansing: A SchoolBook (Ancient Egyptian Literature, Vol. II: The New Kingdom by Miriam Lichtheim)

There's no denying that being in the creative field is challenging. For the most part, you work alone. You're never 100 percent certain that what you have written is as good as you hope it is.

And even if you *are* pretty sure that it is the best piece you've written to date, once it goes out there and then bounces back with great speed and dispatch—and lots of edits!—you start doubting your own judgment and ability.

Public events, especially those with other authors, can be equally intimidating. Over the years, I've participated in a lot of multi-author events, and even though I know that my attention *should* be on the people who are stopping by my table, I can't help but focus on what's happening at the *other* author spaces.

And *that* triggers the age-old comparison contest:

- Why are more people stopping at their tables than at mine?

- Why are people spending more time talking to them than to me?

- Why are their books selling like hotcakes while mine are sitting here like day-old bread?

- In short, why are *they* succeeding and I'm *not*?

How do you counter all those negative emotions that can derail your ability to write? By developing what I call the "5 Cs of Living the Writing Life": confidence, courage, curiosity, commitment and creativity.

1—Build your confidence

Confidence is about having faith in yourself, believing that writing in and of itself is a meaningful endeavor, that you have something important to say, and that you have the ability to say it.

It's not easy to feel confident. Even the best authors doubt their ability to replicate their success. It's not like you can go to the grocery store and buy a pound of inspiration and a quart of creativity and mix it all together to create a final product. Instead, you have to pull all those elements from places that you didn't know existed, combine them in a container, shake the jar and see what comes out.

Then, when what falls on the paper or appears on the monitor isn't at all what you hoped for, you start to worry that the last thing you wrote might very well be the last thing you're *ever* going to write. And your confidence "muscle"—that part of you that you rely on to get you through the writing work—begins to weaken.

In the Writing Roadblocks chapter, I shared some strategies for increasing your confidence level, from creating a Success Résumé to monitoring your self-talk.

Equally important is to stop playing the rating game. The only measuring stick you should be using is one that evaluates your writing ability against what you produced last week, last month, last year. Not the quantity, which can vary depending on a variety of circumstances, but the quality.

When you can see that you are developing your skills as a writer and improving at your craft, then your level of confidence will also grow.

2—Find your courage

No less important to a writer than confidence is the next C: courage. Courage can take many forms and involve a variety of challenges, starting with facing your fear of exploring new writing genres. Perhaps you have focused all of your energy and talent and creativity on one type of writing—for instance, creative nonfiction. Maybe you've even had a few pieces published.

Then someone suggests that you try fiction or poetry, or instead of writing individual short pieces, you should try writing a book. Your knee-jerk response? No way! It's a crazy idea! You already know what you can do. You're comfortable writing in that category or style. You've even had a decent amount of success doing it. Why on earth would you want to set yourself up for potential failure?

Why?

Because you don't know *what* you can do until you *do* it.

Back in December 2009, I found myself in a writing rut or, more precisely, in a not-writing rut. While I loved writing short stories (and had also convinced myself that any fiction beyond 10,000 words was outside my ability), when I looked at my level of production for the past year I realized that I hadn't *done* very much short fiction. Okay, that's not strictly true. Actually, I hadn't written *any* new stories at all. Nothing. Nada.

All I had was a lot of excuses for *not* writing, from increased family responsibilities to a growing client list for my copywriting business. So I made a commitment. Starting January 1, I would set the timer for 30 minutes and before I did anything else, I would write some fiction.

And I did, at first producing just the beginnings of stories that weren't going anywhere, snatches of dialogue with no connection to a plot, and character descriptions that didn't fit in either of the first two categories.

Then, on January 12th, I wrote this:

> *When I was single, I would eat ice cream out of the carton while watching late-night crime drama reruns. Sometimes in the winter, I'd go days, maybe even weeks, without shaving my legs—what did it matter since no one would see the stubble anyway? I'd work out in a stained t-shirt and sweat pants— when I worked out—because, after all, I didn't have to look good for anyone.*
>
> *And I would fantasize about what it would be like to have it all matter—the extra "ice cream pounds," the scratchy legs, the crappy workout outfit— because there was someone in my life who would be looking at me.*

I *thought* I was writing another short story. But by March 13, I had nearly 66,000 words of a novel—my first novel! *How* did that happen? Because I didn't stop writing to *question* my ability to write it. I didn't talk myself out of *continuing* when the word count increased. I didn't *remind* myself that I was a short-story writer, not a novelist.

I found the courage, took the leap and just wrote. It takes courage to move outside your artistic comfort zone, but that is the only way you grow.

Courage is also needed when you are venturing into an emotional territory filled with pain, sorrow or fear.

Another personal story: My mother died in 2005 after a long and difficult struggle with cancer, and I couldn't write about the actual event. Not one word. While my short fiction was filled with stories about loss and grieving, I couldn't write the true story of how that loss affected me: how much I loved her, how much I missed her and what it meant to be motherless.

Or about the last few weeks of her life when my role as caregiver was permeated with fear. Was I meeting her physical and emotional needs? Was there more I should be doing? Was there something I should say—something she needed to hear—before time ran out?

Finally, in 2012, I wrote "Last Words"—an essay exploring my feelings of guilt and remorse for not saying everything that I wished I had before it was too late and my realization that not all communication needs to be verbal. It can also be expressed in action, through the simple touch of a human hand or the look between two people when words are not an option.

It took seven years and a lot of courage for me to go back into that grief-stricken period, but doing so gave me the comfort I needed.

That's the thing about writing: it allows you to explore emotions and events in so many ways if you can just find the courage.

3—Develop your curiosity

The third C—curiosity—is about viewing the world and its inhabitants with the openness of a child. Asking yourself, "What if?" or playing "Let's pretend" as you make your way through the real world, giving your imagination free rein to explore all the possibilities that are behind the reality.

What if that elderly man shuffling down the street wearing worn clothing and carrying a torn shopping bag isn't just one of a thousand poverty-stricken old people but is really a highly successful thief, relying on his appearance to blend into his surroundings?

What if that lovely teenage girl with a blinding white smile isn't the queen of her high school class but the victim of a birth defect that resulted in her inability to do anything more than *just* smile?

What if that woman sitting on a park bench with an empty stroller next to her isn't just *any* mother watching her child playing on a swing set but a mother who has lost her only child and can only find comfort around other children?

That's one of the reasons why I like to fly. I sit in the terminal and watch people interact, eavesdrop on their conversation—I know, bad girl—and then the wheels start turning and I make up story lines in my head.

Even if your preferred writing form deals with fact, not fiction, you still need curiosity coupled with imagination and empathy to fully understand those about whom you write. While you may have a lot of background information and facts about the person or the situation, you still require a well-developed sense of inquisitiveness to discover what you *don't* know. Otherwise, your preconceptions can inhibit your ability to gain a deeper understanding of the circumstances and events, the motivations and *results* of those motivations.

Your writing ability will only develop if you allow yourself to be curious—about the world, about events, about people.

4—Ignite your creativity

From *feeling* a sense of curiosity to wanting to *act* on that curiosity—that is the spark that ignites the next C: creativity. Creativity is about wanting to bring something new to light, wanting to bring an unborn character to life, wanting to satisfy that desire to use words to illuminate a hitherto hidden truth. It's a necessary quality for a writer. But sometimes those creative fires can look more like cold ashes.

You want to write. You have to write. There is a burning deep inside of you that demands that you write. Those are the wonderful days when you can't wait to get to the computer or paper, when the hours fly by while you are caught up in what you are writing.

And then there are the *other* times, the times when you hit an inspirational dry spell. You're ready to write, you have time to write, but you are suffering from an internal blockage I refer to as "creative constipation."

You are, quite simply, stuck. So what do you do?

- Stare at the monitor screen, hoping that words will magically appear?

- Pick up the pencil or place your fingers on the keyboard, hoping that the physical connection will result in literary output?

- Call a fellow writer and whine about how hard it is to be a writer, how no one understands the exhausting process of turning out miles of sentences and mountains of paragraphs?

You can do any or all of the above. I certainly have. Unfortunately, none of those responses is likely to turn cold ashes into warm embers or warm embers into a glowing flame.

As Jack London said in his article, "Getting Into Print" that appeared in *The Editor* in 1903, "Don't loaf and invite inspiration; light out after it with a club," and that's equally true of creativity. If you wait until you *feel* creative, chances are you are in for a good long wait.

Instead, you need to find methods that will fan those creative fires. For some, that's putting on certain types of music. Visuals can also help. Working on a historical piece? Surround yourself with images from that time, suggested historical novelist Marie Lavender.

"I spend lots of time combing through old photographs or pictures of a location to get a real feel for the place, anything that will inspire me to write, to better describe the way a character feels when he or she encounters something," she said. She recommended that writers "collect photographs that really tell a story about a place, a person or thing. Get in touch with the details."

Easily distracted? You may need to have a room with no images at all, like author Josh Barkan, who prefers "places that have no noise, and also that have almost no decoration. The ideal place for me to write is a place with a white wall in front of me."

Alternatively, shake up your writing routine: write on paper instead of electronically, or randomly choose a part of your project to work on instead of working from page one to the end. It's all about finding what works for you, and that can vary depending on the type of project and your current circumstances.

And while it's true that you shouldn't "sit around and wait," it can help to know when your right brain is at its peak operating state. I'm a morning person, so that's when I "birth" new pieces: articles, essays, fiction. But your creative fires might blaze better at night. In that case, adjust your schedule, resist the lure of entertainment and get to your writing.

Whatever it is that is keeping your creative fires from burning as hotly as they should, deal with it so you can keep writing.

5—Make your commitment

"This year I'm going to make time to write every day." Then, two days, two weeks, two months later, your "time to write" has been pushed aside for all those other pressing and urgent items on your schedule. Does that sound familiar?

In all the years I have been interviewing writers, I can count on the fingers of one hand the number who said they have plenty of time to write. For the rest of them, finding writing time is a daily struggle.

Now I will grant you that life can get crazy and unexpected responsibilities can crop up, and at times we have to put our writing on the back burner. But if you see that it's happening more often than not, the problem may not be a lack of time but the last C: commitment.

For some, it's feeling that choosing to write is selfish or a waste of time, either because it may not bring in any money or because they don't believe they are "real writers" and so don't deserve to make writing time a priority.

But it isn't being published that makes you a writer. You are a writer as long as you write. If you have the desire and the ability to write, you owe it to yourself to make the commitment to do so.

Now let's talk about the other commitment: to write the best possible piece you can.

Writing isn't easy. Even for fiction, there may be a certain amount of research called for, some fact-finding required, something beyond using your software program's thesaurus to find the right word or phrase. There are no shortcuts to writing well. It takes time, energy, a willingness to get feedback and then revise as needed based on that feedback.

If you want to write the best possible piece you can, then you have to be willing to give it the time it needs and, if necessary, to improve your writing skills so you can deliver.

At the end of her short story collection, *Come Along With Me*, Shirley Jackson included her "Notes for a Young Writer"—advice intended for those writing short fiction but easily applicable to those working in other genres as well.

Among her words of wisdom is the admonition that your story (or article or essay) is essentially a bargain with your reader, and, she noted, an uneasy one at that. Your part is to keep your readers interested while their role is to keep reading.

It's a sacred trust you have with your readers. They are giving you their time, and you need to deliver something worthy of it. It doesn't matter if it's a serious work or a lighthearted beach read. It should still be as good as it can be.

Your job as a writer is not to look for ways to lower the bar but to constantly be striving to raise it, exceed it, and then raise it yet again.

That is the commitment you have to your readers, to yourself, and to writing.

The 5 Cs of Living the Writing Life

- **Confidence**—Having faith in yourself. Believing that this is a meaningful endeavor, that you have something important to say, and that you have the ability to say it.

- **Courage**—Not being afraid to push your abilities to the fullest or venture into a territory filled with pain, sorrow or fear.

- **Curiosity**—Viewing the world and its inhabitants with the openness of a child, asking yourself, "What if?" or playing "Let's pretend" to allow yourself to explore other possibilities.

- **Creativity**—Wanting to bring something new to light, wanting to bring an unborn character to life.

- **Commitment**—Making writing an important part of your life and making a commitment to your reader: to write the best possible piece you can.

CITATIONS

THE POWER OF PASSION

Gold by Isaac Asimov (Harper Voyager; Reprint edition, 2003)

"How to sell loads of books" by Russell Blake (Russell Blake website: russellblake.com/how-to-sell-loads-of-books/)

WHAT'S YOUR RUT?

The Courage to Write by Ralph Keyes (Henry Holt and Company, 1995)

Sally Koslow (Sally Koslow website: sallykoslow.com/content/author.asp)

"Can authors be successful in multiple genres?" by Joanna Penn (The Creative Penn website: www.thecreativepenn.com/2009/04/25/can-authors-be-successful-in-multiple-genres/)

"The Pros and Cons of Switching Genres" by Summerita Rhayne (Jami Gold's website: jamigold.com/2014/11/the-pros-and-cons-of-switching-genres-guest-summerita-rhayne/)

"The rise of climate fiction: When literature takes on global warming and devastating droughts" by Michael Berry (Salon: www.salon.com/2014/10/26/the_rise_of

_climate_fiction_when_literature_takes_on_global_warming_
and_devastating_droughts/)

"Should You Write Under A Pen Name?" By Paige Duke (Standout
Books website: www.standoutbooks.com/write-pen-name/)

YOUR WRITING ROAD MAP

"The Top 7 Benefits of Writing Down Your Goals" by Sooraj
Singh (Get Motivation blog: www.getmotivation.com/
motivationblog/2015/01/the-top-7-benefits
-of-writing-down-your-goals/)

"10 Guidelines for Effective Goal Setting" by Adam Hodges
(Training Peaks: www.trainingpeaks.com/blog/10-guidelines
-for-effective-goal-setting/)

"Time Management for Authorpreneurs" by Sharon C.
Jenkins (The Writer's Place: www.nancychristie.com/
writersplace/2017/05/09/time-management-for-
authorpreneurs-guest-post-by-sharon-c-jenkins/)

RAISING THE BAR

On Writing – A Memoir of the Craft by Stephen King (Pocket
Books, 2001)

IT'S ALL ABOUT CONNECTIONS

"Writing Groups 101: How to Find Your Perfect Match" by
Kristen Pope (The Write Life website: thewritelife.com/
writing-groups-101/)

"9 tips for squeezing more out of a writers' conference" by
Michelle Rafter (Michelle Rafter website: michellerafter.
com/2015/04/26/8-tips-to-get-the-most-out-of-attending-
a-writers-conference/)

"How To Choose A Writing Conference" by Erika Dreifus (Erika Dreifus website: www.erikadreifus.com/resources/conferences-centers/)

THE MONEY ISSUE

Robert Benchley ("Quotations from Robert Benchley": www.robertbenchley.org/sob/quotes.htm)

"If You Insist on Having Writer's Block, Here's Help" by Larry Kahaner (The Non-Fiction Novelist blog: nonfictionnovelist.wordpress.com/2014/09/22/if-you-insist-on-having-writers-block-heres-help/)

"Billy Joel on Not Working and Not Giving Up Drinking" by Andrew Goldman (*New York Times Magazine*: www.nytimes.com/2013/05/26/magazine/billy-joel-on-not-working-and-not-giving-up-drinking.html)

THANKS, BUT NO THANKS

Isaac Asimov ("12 Famous Writers on Literary Rejection": www.aerogrammestudio.com/2013/06/15/12-famous-writers-on-literary-rejection)

"Famous Author Rejection Letters: True Stories Of Unbelievable Rejections" (Writer's Relief website: writersrelief.com/blog/2011/07/famous-author-rejection-letters/)

William Zinsser (*The Resilient Writer* by Catherine Wald, Persea Books, Inc., 2005)

Stephen King (*On Writing*, Pocket Books, 2000)

"What Editors Want: A Must-Read for Writers Submitting to Literary Magazines" by Lynne Barrett (The Review Review website: www.thereviewreview.net/publishing-tips/what-editors-want-must-read-writers-submitti)

"Is rejection your fault? Or theirs?" by Mridu Khullar Relph (The International Freelancer newsletter: us6. campaign-archive1.com/home/?u=b31f174bfe74fa 8b2cb2d7e01&id=8c4be28f73)

"Why You Should Aim For 100 Rejections A Year" by Kim Liao (LitHub website: lithub.com/ why-you-should-aim-for-100-rejections-a-year/)

Barbara Kingsolver ("12 Famous Writers on Literary Rejection": www. aerogrammestudio.com/2013/06/15/12-famous-writ-ers-on-literary-rejection)

WRITING ROADBLOCKS

"The Ideal Work Schedule, as Determined by Circadian Rhythms" by Christopher M. Barnes (*Harvard Business Review*: hbr. org/2015/01/the-ideal-work-schedule-as-determined-by-circadian-rhythms)

"How To Achieve Peak Productivity Levels, Even While Procrastinating" by Elena Bajic (*Forbes*: www.forbes.com/ sites/elenabajic/2016/01/17/how-to-achieve-peak-produc-tivity-levels-even-while-procrastinating/#197b4f925dc2)

"Time of day effects on problem solving: When the non-optimal is optimal" by Mareike B. Wieth and Rose T. Zacks (*Thinking & Reasoning*, Volume 17, 2011: www.tandfonline.com/doi/ful l/10.1080/13546783.2011.625663)

The Seven Habits of Highly Effective People by Stephen Covey (A Fireside Book, 1989)

"13 Quirky Workplaces of Famous Writers" by Zachary Petit (*Writer's Digest*: www.writersdigest.com/editor-blogs/ there-are-no-rules/13-quirky-workplaces-of-famous-writers)

"Brooklyn novelist Peter Brett found his muse and wrote first novel commuting on the F line" by Erin Durkin (*New York Daily News*: www.nydailynews.com/new-york/brooklyn/brooklyn-novelist-peter-brett-found-muse-wrote-commuting-f-line-article-1.362398)

"How To Write a Novel on Your Commute" by Jonathan Stone (*Writer's Digest*: www.writersdigest.com/online-editor/how-to-write-a-novel-on-your-commute)

"Smartphone author writes novel on commute" by Olivia Wannan (Stuff website: www.stuff.co.nz/entertainment/books/8505693/Smartphone-author-writes-novel-on-commute)

"23 Timeless Quotes About Writing" by Brian A. Klems (*Writer's Digest*: www.writersdigest.com/whats-new/23-timeless-quotes-about-writing)

"Neuroscience of Creativity" (YorkPsych website: appsychtextbk.wikispaces.com/Neuroscience+of+Creativity)

"Regular Exercise Could Boost Creativity" (Huffington Post website: www.huffingtonpost.com/2013/12/09/exercise-creativity-physical-activity_n_4394310.html)

The Artist's Way: A Spiritual Path to Higher Creativity by Julia Cameron with Mark Bryan (Jeremy P. Tarcher/Putnam Book, 1992)

"The impact of physical exercise on convergent and divergent thinking" by Lorenza S. Colzato, Ayca Szapora, Justine N. Pannekoek and Bernhard Hommel (*Frontiers in Human Neuroscience*: journal.frontiersin.org/article/10.3389/fnhum.2013.00824/full)

"Lacking inspiration? Exercise found to boost creativity" by Sarah Knapton (*The Telegraph*: www.telegraph.co.uk/news/science/

science-news/10491702/Lacking-inspiration-Exercise-found-to-boost-creativity.html)

"Stanford study finds walking improves creativity" by May Wong (*Stanford News*: news.stanford.edu/2014/04/24/walking-vs-sitting-042414/)

"Give Your Ideas Some Legs: The Positive Effect of Walking on Creative Thinking" by Marily Oppezzo and Daniel L. Schwartz, Stanford University (*Journal of Experimental Psychology*: www.apa.org/pubs/journals/releases/xlm-a0036577.pdf)

"How Exercise Makes You More Creative" by Sally Koslow (Health.com: www.health.com/health/article/0,,20412092,00.html)

"Training your brain for creativity" by James S. Fell (*Chicago Tribune*: articles.chicagotribune.com/2014-03-14/health/sc-health-0312-fitness-creative-decision-making-20140312_1_creativity-treadmill-environment)

"Aerobic Exercise and Cognitive Creativity: Immediate and Residual Effects" by David M. Blanchette, Stephen P. Ramocki, John N. O'del, and Michael S. Casey (*Creativity Research Journal*: www.tandfonline.com/doi/abs/10.1080/10400419.2005.9651483)

"Is Noise Always Bad? Exploring the Effects of Ambient Noise on Creative Cognition" by Ravi Mehta, Rui (Juliet) Zhu, and Amar Cheema (*Journal of Consumer Research*: www.jstor.org/stable/10.1086/665048)

"How To Always Have Something Awesome To Write About" by Paige Duke (Standout Books website: www.standoutbooks.com/awesome-inspiration-muse/)

THE PROCRASTINATION PREDICAMENT

Ben Franklin (*Poor Richard Improved, 1758*: founders.archives. gov/documents/Franklin/01-07-02-0146)

Thomas Edison (Thomas Edison website: thomasedison.com/ quotes.html)

"10 Foolproof Tips for Overcoming Procrastination" by Dr. Jeremy Dean (PsyBlog blog: www.spring.org.uk/2014/03/10-fool-proof-tips-for-overcoming-procrastination.php)

Write Away by Elizabeth George (HarperCollins, 2004)

"Procrastination" (The Writing Center at UNC-Chapel Hill web-site: writingcenter.unc.edu/handouts/procrastination/)

CREATING YOUR WRITING SPACE

"40 Inspiring Workspaces Of The Famously Creative" by Summer Anne Burton (Buzzfeed: www.buzzfeed.com/summeran-ne/40-inspiring-workspaces-of-the-famously-creative)

"Color Theory for Designers, Part 1: The Meaning of Color" by Cameron Chapman (*Smashing Magazine*: www.smashing magazine.com/2010/01/color-theory-for-designers -part-1-the-meaning-of-color/)

"The Writing Space of famous writers" (Booktique blog: booktique. weebly.com/blog/the-writing-space-of-famous-writers)

Agatha Christie: An Autobiography by Agatha Christie (HarperCollins, 2011)

A Room of One's Own by Virginia Woolf (Harcourt, Brace, Jovanovich, 1929)

"What are the characteristics of color?" (Pantone website: www. pantone.com/what-are-the-characteristics-of-color)

"What is color temperature?" (Westinghouse website: www. westinghouselighting.com/color-temperature.aspx)

YOUR WRITING TOOLBOX

Agatha Christie: An Autobiography by Agatha Christie (HarperCollins, 2011)

"6 Scents That Can Transform Your Mood and Productivity" by Lisa Evans (Entrepreneur.com: www.entrepreneur.com/ article/224575)

"Aromatherapy Scents to Increase Productivity" by Kayla Matthews (Productivity Theory website: productivitytheory. com/10-aromatherapy-scents-to-increase-productivity/)

"7 Scents That Boost Productivity And Help You Focus— Even When You're Exhausted" by Allison Young (Rodale's *Organic Life* website: www.rodalesorganiclife.com/wellbeing/ best-scents-for-productivity-and-focus/slide/2)

"Saints' Names: Patrons of the Arts–Cecilia, Clare and Celestine" (Nameberry.com: nameberry.com/blog/ saints-names-patrons-of-the-arts-cecilia-clare-and-celestine)

"List of knowledge deities" (Wikipedia: en.wikipedia.org/wiki/ List_of_knowledge_deities)

Ancient Egypt Online (www.ancientegyptonline.co.uk/ seshat.html)

"Gods and Goddesses" (Earthchild Pendants website: www. earthchildpendants.co.uk/gods.html)

"Turn It Up: How the Right Amount of Ambient Noise Increases Creativity" by Dave Burkus (99u: 99u.com/articles/16711/ turn-it-up-how-the-right-about-of-ambient-noise-increases-creativity)

"Is Noise Always Bad? Exploring the Effects of Ambient Noise on Creative Cognition" by Ravi Mehta, Rui (Juliet) Zhu and Amar Cheema (*Journal of Consumer Research*: www.jstor.org/ stable/10.1086/665048)

"How Does Scent Drive Human Behavior?" by Christopher Bergland (*Psychology Today*: www. psychologytoday.com/blog/the-athletes-way/201506/ how-does-scent-drive-human-behavior)

"Brain Basics: Know Your Brain" (education.ninds.nih.gov/ brochures/brain_basics_know_your_brain-508.pdf)

Chapter 6. Limbic System: Amygdala by Anthony Wright, Ph.D. (Neuroscience Online: neuroscience.uth.tmc.edu/s4/ chapter06.html)

Review Of Clinical And Functional Neuroscience –Chapter 9– Limbic System (Dartmouth Medical School: www.dartmouth. edu/~rswenson/NeuroSci/chapter_9.html)

The Artist's Way: A Spiritual Path to Higher Creativity by Julia Cameron with Mark Bryan (Jeremy P. Tarcher/Putnam Book, 1992)

The Limbic System by Matthew Dahlitz (*The Neuropsychotherapist*: www.neuropsychotherapist.com/the-limbic-system/)

LIVING THE WRITING LIFE

Ancient Egyptian Literature: A Book of Readings. Volume 2: The New Kingdom by Miriam Lichtheim (University of California Press, 1976)

"Jack London's Candid 1903 Advice to Writers Trying to Get Into Print" by Rebecca Onion ("Getting into Print," *The Editor* magazine, 1903: www.slate.com/blogs/the_vault/2015/07/20/jack_london_the_author_s_writing_advice.html)

Come Along With Me by Shirley Jackson (Penguin Books, 1995)

RESOURCES

Books

101 Tips for Becoming a $100,000-a-Year Freelance Writer by Dawn Josephson (Ground Rules Press, 2014)

13 Ways to Get the Writing Done Faster: Two pro writers share their secrets (Make a Living Writing) by Linda Formichelli and Carol Tice (TiceWrites LLC, 2012)

30 Perfect Days, Finding Abundance in Ordinary Life by Claudia Taller (Igniting Possibilities Press, 2014)

50 Things to Know About Writing for a Living: How You Can Make Money Writing by Amanda Walton (CZYK Publishing, 2014)

500 Writing Prompts (Piccadilly Books, 2015)

Agatha Christie: An Autobiography by Agatha Christie (HarperCollins, 2011)

Are You a Super Author? 14 Stories of Super Authors Who Have Mastered Authorpreneurship by Sharon C. Jenkins (CreateSpace Independent Publishing Platform, 2017)

Author 101 Bestselling Book Publicity: The Insider's Guide to Promoting Your Book—and Yourself by Rick Frishman, Robyn Freedman Spizman and Mark Steisel (Adams Media, 2nd edition, 2006)

Author 101: Bestselling Secrets from Top Agents by Rick Frishman, Robyn Freedman Spizman and Mark Steisel (Adams Media, 2nd edition, 2005)

Authorpreneurship: The Business Start-Up Manual for Authors by Sharon C. Jenkins (CreateSpace Independent Publishing Platform, 2014)

Bird by Bird: Some Instructions on Writing and Life by Anne Lamott (Anchor, 1995)

Blogging Basics for Authors: 30 Lessons to Help Writers Create Effective Blogs and Blog Content by Nina Amir (Pure Spirit Creations, 2015)

Christian Authorpreneurship, Mastering the Business of Writing by Sharon C. Jenkins (The Authorpreneurship Project, 2016)

Create A Character Clinic: A Step-By-Step Course in Creating Deeper, Better Fictional People by Holly Lisle (Holly Lisle; 2nd edition, 2013)

Creative Visualization for Writers: An Interactive Guide for Bringing Your Book Ideas and Your Writing Career to Life by Nina Amir (Writer's Digest Books; Csm edition, 2016)

FEAR NOT! Confidence-Building Insights, Tips, and Techniques for Freelance Writers (Make a Living Writing Book 3) by Carol Tice, Goldie Ector, Amy Dunn Muscoso, Ivy Sheldon, Jessi Stanley, Nillu Nasser Stelter and Steph Weber (TiceWrites LLC, 2015)

Fierce on The Page: Become the Writer You Were Meant to Be and Succeed on Your Own Terms by Sage Cohen (Writer's Digest Books, 2016)

Freelance Business Bootcamp: How to Launch, Earn, and Grow into a Well-Paid Freelancer (Freelance Writers Den Book 4) by Carol Tice and Neil Tortorella (TiceWrites LLC, 2014)

Get Your Book in the News: How to Write a Press Release That Announces Your Book by Sandra Beckwith (Beckwith Communications, 2013)

Gold by Isaac Asimov (Harper Voyager, Reprint edition, 2003)

How to Avoid 101 Book Publishing Blunders, Bloopers and Boo-Boos by Judith Briles (Mile High Press, 2016)

How to Be a Well-Paid Freelance Blogger: Earn $50-$100 a Post and More (Freelance Writers Den) by Carol Tice (TiceWrites LLC, 2014)

How to Blog a Book Revised and Expanded Edition: Write, Publish, and Promote Your Work One Post at a Time by Nina Amir (Writer's Digest Books; Revised Edition, 2015)

How to Get Great Freelance Clients: Learn how to earn more—find quality clients and get the gig (Freelance Writers Den Book 3) by Carol Tice (TiceWrites LLC, 2014)

How to Open and Operate a Home-Based Writing Business by Lucy V. Parker (Globe Pequot Press, 1994)

If You Want to Write: A Book about Art, Independence and Spirit by Brenda Ueland (Graywolf Press, 2nd edition, 2007)

Lifelong Writing Habit: The Secret To Writing Every Day (Write Faster, Write Smarter) (Volume 2) by Chris Fox (CreateSpace Independent Publishing Platform, 2015)

Magazine Queries That Worked: Build Income and Authority With Freelance Journalism by Tara Lynne Groth (Amazon Digital Services LLC, 2017)

Make A REAL LIVING as a Freelance Writer: How To Win Top Writing Assignments by Jenna Glatzer (Nomad Press, 2004)

Making a Literary Life: Advice for Writers and Other Dreamers by Carolyn See (Ballantine Books, Reprint edition, 2003)

Make Money As A Freelance Writer: 7 Simple Steps to Start Your Freelance Writing Business and Earn Your First $1,000 by Sally Miller and Gina Horkey (Amazon Digital Services LLC, 2016)

Negotiating With the Dead: A Writer on Writing by Margaret Atwood (Anchor, 2003)

On Writing – A Memoir of the Craft by Stephen King (Pocket Books, 2001)

On Writing Well: The Classic Guide to Writing Nonfiction by William Zinsser (Harper Perennial, 30th Anniversary Edition, 2016)

Outwitting Writer's Block: And Other Problems of the Pen by Jenna Glatzer (Lyons Press, 1st edition, 2003)

Publishing 101: A First-Time Author's Guide to Getting Published, Marketing and Promoting Your Book, and Building a Successful Career by Jane Friedman (MBA for Writers, 1st edition, 2014)

Scratch: Writers, Money, and the Art of Making a Living by Manjula Martin (Simon & Schuster, 2017)

Secrets of a Freelance Writer: How to Make $100,000 a Year or More by Robert W. Bly (Holt Paperbacks, 2006)

Self-Promotion for the Creative Person by Lee Silber (Crown Business, 2001)

Self-Publishing Books 101: A Step-by-Step Guide to Publishing Your Book in Multiple Formats (Author 101 Series, Volume 1) by Shelley Hitz (Body and Soul Publishing, 2014)

Shut Up and Write: The No-Nonsense, No B.S. Guide to Getting Words on the Page by Mridu Khullar Relph (Amazon Digital Services LLC, 2016)

Small Blog, Big Income: Advanced Ninja Tricks for Profitable Blogging: With Special Report: 90 Tips to Make Money Blogging by Carol Tice (TiceWrites LLC, 2016)

Small Blog, Big Income: One Niche Blogger's 7 Step Success Formula by Carol Tice (TiceWrites LLC, 2016)

Social Media Just for Writers: How to Build Your Online Platform and Find and Engage with Your Readers by Frances Caballo (ACT Communications, 2nd edition, 2017)

Start & Run a Copywriting Business (Start & Run Business Series) by Steve Slaunwhite (Self-Counsel Press, 2nd edition, 2005)

Start Here: 40 Freelance Writers Share How They Find Clients, Stay Motivated & Earn Well Today (Make a Living Writing Book 2) by Carol Tice, Carol J. Alexander, Bryan Collins, Nicole Dieker, David Leonhardt, Cinthia Ritchie and Allen Taylor (TiceWrites LLC, 2015)

Still Writing: The Perils and Pleasures of a Creative Life by Dani Shapiro (Grove Press, 2014)

The $100,000 Writer by Nancy Flynn (Adams Media Corporation, 2000)

The 3 A.M. Epiphany by Brian Kiteley (Writer's Digest Books, 2005)

The 4 A.M. Breakthrough by Brian Kiteley (Writer's Digest Books, 2009)

The Artist's Way: A Spiritual Path to Higher Creativity by Julia Cameron with Mark Bryan (Jeremy P. Tarcher/Putnam Book, 1992)

The Audacity to be a Writer: 50 Inspiring Articles on Writing that Could Change Your Life by Bryan Hutchinson (CreateSpace Independent Publishing Platform, 2015)

The Author Training Manual: Develop Marketable Ideas, Craft Books That Sell, Become the Author Publishers Want, and Self-Publish Effectively by Nina Amir and James Scott Bell (Writer's Digest Books, 2014)

The Author's Guide to Goodreads: How to Engage with Readers and Market Your Books by Frances Caballo (ACT Communications, 1st edition, 2016)

The Courage to Write by Ralph Keyes (Henry Holt and Company, 1995)

The Elements of Style, Fourth Edition by William Strunk Jr., E. B. White (Pearson, 1999)

The Everything Guide To Writing Copy: From Ads and Press Release to On-Air and Online Promos–All You Need to Create Copy That Sells by Steve Slaunwhite (Everything, 2007)

The Forest for the Trees (Revised and Updated): An Editor's Advice to Writers by Betsy Lerner (Riverhead Books, 2010)

The Freelance Writer's Handbook by Gary Provost (Crossroad Press; Crossroad Press Digital Edition, 2015)

The Freelance Writer's Guide to Making $1,000 More This Month by Mridu Khullar Relph (Amazon Digital Services LLC, 2014)

The Mental Game of Writing: How to Overcome Obstacles, Stay Creative and Productive and Free Your Mind for Success by James Scott Bell (Compendium Press, 2016)

The Novel Pitch: Everything You Need to Know to Write a Successful Query for Your Fiction by Ann Henry (CreateSpace Independent Publishing Platform, 2016)

The Pocket Small Business Owner's Guide to Starting Your Business on a Shoestring (Pocket Small Business Owner's Guides) by Carol Tice (Allworth Press, 1st edition, 2013)

The Proust Effect: The Senses as Doorways to Lost Memories by Cretien van Campen (OUP Oxford, 1st edition, 2014)

The Renegade Writer: A Totally Unconventional Guide to Freelance Writing Success by Linda Formichelli and Diana Burrell (Renegade Writer Press, 2017)

The Resilient Writer: Tales of Rejection and Triumph by 23 Top Authors by Catherine Wald (Persea Books, Inc., 2005)

The Step-by-Step Guide to Freelance Writing Success: How to Break In and Start Earning—Fast! (Freelance Writers Den Book 2) by Carol Tice and Laura Spencer (TiceWrites LLC, 2014)

The Street Smart Writer: Self Defense Against Sharks and Scams in the Writing World by Jenna Glatzer and Daniel Steven (Nomad Press, 2006)

The Way of the Writer: Reflections on the Art and Craft of Storytelling by Charles Johnson (Scribner, Reprint edition, 2016)

The Wealthy Freelancer by Steve Slaunwhite, Pete Savage and Ed Gandia (ALPHA, 2010)

The Wealthy Writer by Michael Meanwell (Writer's Digest Books, 2004)

The Well-Fed Writer by Peter Bowerman (Fanove Publishing, 2009)

The World Split Open: Great Authors on How and Why We Write (A Literary Arts Reader) by Margaret Atwood, Russell Banks, Ursula K. Le Guin, Marilynne Robinson, Wallace Stegner, Robert Stone and Jeanette Winterson (Tin House Books, 1st edition, 2014)

The Writer on Her Work, edited by Janet Sternburg (Norton, 1981)

The Writer's Idea Book by Jack Heffron (Writer's Digest Books, 10 Anv. Edition, 2012)

The Writer's Hand Journals: Character Journal: 100 of the best character descriptions from favorite authors, old and new! (Volume 1) by Dawn Reno Langley (CreateSpace Independent Publishing Platform, 1st edition, 2016)

The Writer's Hand Journals: Meditations: 100 Inspiring Quotes from all Religions (The Writer's Hand Journals) (Volume 3) by Dawn Reno Langley (CreateSpace Independent Publishing Platform, 1st edition, 2016)

The Writer's Hand Journals: Setting/Place: 100 Quotes Depicting Setting in your Favorite Novels to Inspire You! (Volume 2) by Dawn Reno Langley (CreateSpace Independent Publishing Platform, 1st edition, 2016)

The Writer's Hand Journals: Words of Love (Volume 4) by Dawn Reno Langley (CreateSpace Independent Publishing Platform, 1st edition, 2017)

The Writer's Process: Getting Your Brain in Gear by Anne Janzer (Cuesta Park Consulting, 2016)

The Writing Life by Annie Dillard (Harper Perennial, 2013)

The Writing Life edited by Marie Arana (Public Affairs, 1st edition, 2003)

Thinking Like Your Editor: How to Write Great Serious Nonfiction and Get It Published by Susan Rabiner and Alfred Fortunato (W. W. Norton & Company, Reprint edition, 2003)

Using Periscope to #CreateBookBuzz by Sharon C. Jenkins (Ellechor Media & Associates, LLC, 2016)

Using Periscope to Master Authorpreneurship by Sharon C. Jenkins(Ellechor Media& Associates, LLC, 2015)

What Editors Want: A Must-Read for Writers Submitting to Literary Magazines by Lynne Barrett (Rain Chain Press, 1st edition, 2016)

Why We Write: 20 Acclaimed Authors on How and Why They Do What They Do edited by Meredith Maran (Plume, 2013)

Why Write?: A Master Class on the Art of Writing and Why it Matters by Mark Edmundson (Bloomsbury USA, 2016)

Words You Thought You Knew: 1001 Commonly Misused and Misunderstood Words and Phrases by Jenna Glatzer (Adams Media Corporation, 2003)

Write Away by Elizabeth George (HarperCollins, 2004)

Write For Your Life: The Home Seminar for Writers by Lawrence Block (CreateSpace Independent Publishing Platform, 2014)

Write. Publish. Repeat.: The No-Luck-Required Guide to Self-Publishing Success by Sean Platt and Johnny B. Truant (Sterling & Stone, 2015)

Writer With a Day Job by Aine Greaney (Writer's Digest Books, 2011)

Writer's Market (Writer's Digest Books, annual publication)

Writerpreneur: How to Work From Home as an Online Writer, Find Premium Clients, & Make Money by Rory Parker (Gordon Road Publishing House, 2012)

Writing the Mind Alive: The Proprioceptive Method For Finding Your Authentic Voice by Linda Trichter Metcalf, Ph.D. (Ballantine Books, 2002)

Writing Tools: 55 Essential Strategies for Every Writer by Roy Peter Clark (Little, Brown and Company, 1st edition, 2008)

Your First 1000 Copies: The Step-by-Step Guide to Marketing Your Book by Tim Grahl (Out:think, 1st Edition, 2013)

Zen in the Art of Writing by Ray Bradbury (Bantam Book, 1992)

Writing Locations and Opportunities

Artist-in-Residence (AIR) programs, National Park Service (www.nps.gov/subjects/arts/air.htm)

The Poynter Institute, St. Petersburg, Florida (www.poynter.org/)

Sterling Room for Writers, Multnomah County Library, Portland, Oregon (multcolib.org/library-location/sterling-room-writers)

The Center for Fiction, Mercantile Library, New York City, New York (centerforfiction.org/)

The Writers' Room of Boston, Boston, Massachusetts (www.writersroomofboston.org)

The Writing Center at UNC-Chapel Hill (writingcenter.unc.edu/)

William N. Skirball Writers' Center, Cuyahoga County Public Library, South Euclid, Ohio (www.cuyahogalibrary.org/Services/William-N-Skirball-Writers-Center.aspx)

Writer's Rooms, Nashville Public Library, Nashville, Tennessee (library.nashville.org/about/policies/writers-rooms-guidelines)

Conferences and Workshops

Note: These are just a few of the many writing conferences, workshops and book fairs. For more information, visit AWP Writer's Calendar (www.awpwriter.org/community_calendar/writers_calendar), Everfest's Book Festivals (www.everfest.com/

book-festivals) and ShawGuides' Guide to Writers Conferences & Writing Workshops (writing.shawguides.com/).

Association of Writers & Writing Programs—AWP Conference & Bookfair (www.awpwriter.org/awp_conference/overview): The AWP Conference & Bookfair is an essential annual destination for writers, teachers, students, editors, and publishers. The conference features over 2,000 presenters and 550 readings, panels, and craft lectures. The bookfair hosted over 800 presses, journals, and literary organizations from around the world. AWP's is now the largest literary conference in North America.

Gotham Writers Workshops (www.writingclasses.com/): Gotham Writers Workshop is a creative home in New York City and Online where writers develop their craft and come together in the spirit of discovery and fellowship.

Grub Street's Muse and the Marketplace (museandthemarketplace.com/): A three-day literary conference that gives aspiring writers a better understanding of the craft of fiction and nonfiction, prepares them for the ever-changing world of publishing and promotion, and creates opportunities for meaningful networking.

International Women's Writing Guild Conferences (iwwg.wildapricot.org/): Regional and national conferences featuring workshops on a wide range of topics and "Meet the Agents" one-on-one sessions to pitch your work.

The Writing Center of the Writing University (writingcenter.uiowa.edu): The Writing Center assists with all writing projects, including multimedia projects, at any stage of development. Our services are free and available to anyone in the University of Iowa community.

University of Iowa Writers' Workshop (writersworkshop.uiowa. edu/): The University of Iowa Writers' Workshop (known informally as the Iowa Writers' Workshop) was the first creative writing degree program in the United States, and since its founding in 1936, the program has been home to thousands of remarkable writers.

The Writer's Digest Annual Conference (www.writersdigestconference.com/): Held every August in Midtown New York, is one of the largest gatherings of its kind, in 2016 drawing some 1,000 writers, editors, agents and other publishing professionals to gather and offer instruction and inspiration to aspiring and working writers alike.

Willamette Writers Conference (willamettewriters.org/wwcon/): Willamette Writers Conference features teachers, speakers, writers, agents, editors and producers as well as other industry professionals from across North America to create a world-class curriculum for beginning and advanced writers alike.

Websites/Blogs/Newsletters

All Freelance Writing (allfreelancewriting.com/ freelance-hourly-rate-calculator/)

Erika Dreifus (www.erikadreifus.com/)

Freelance Writing (www.freelancewriting.com/)

Funds for Writers (fundsforwriters.com/)

Goodreads (www.goodreads.com/)

Gotham Writers (www.writingclasses.com/classes/online)

The International Freelancer (www.theinternationalfreelancer.com/)

Jane Friedman (janefriedman.com/)

LibraryThing (www.librarything.com/)

Make a Living Writing (www.makealivingwriting.com/)

Massachusetts Institute of Technology's OpenCourseWare (ocw. mit.edu/about/)

Master Class (www.masterclass.com/)

New Pages (www.newpages.com/magazines)

Online Writing Lab (OWL) at Purdue University (owl.english. purdue.edu/owl/)

Poets & Writers magazine "Live" (www.pw.org/live)

Profitable Copy (www.profitable-copy.com/)

Stanford University's Stanford Online (online.stanford.edu/about)

The ASJA Weekly (www.multibriefs.com/briefs/asja/ ASJA122013.php)

The Creative Penn (www.thecreativepenn.com/)

The International Freelancer (www.TheInternationalFreelancer.com)

The Renegade Writer (www.therenegadewriter.com/)

The Well-Fed Writer (www.wellfedwriter.com /)

The Write Direction: Freelance Copywriting Fee Schedule (writedirection.com/fee-schedule/)

The Write Practice (thewritepractice.com/)

The Writer magazine's Writing Program listing (www.writermag. com/market-directory/writing-program/)

Word Count: Freelancing in the Digital Age (michellerafter.com/)

Write Naked (www.taralynnegroth.com/newsletter-for-writers.html)

Writer's Digest free weekly e-newsletter (www.writersdigest.com/subscribe/free-weekly-newsletter)

Writer's Digest magazine's webinars (www.writersdigest.com/free-book-webinars)

Writers Weekly (www.writersweekly.com/)

Writing Assistance, Inc. (www.writingassist.com/)

Writing-World.com (www.writing-world.com/)

Writing Organizations

Note: These are just a few of the many organizations for writers. For more information, visit Writers and Editors' "Major writers organizations" (www.writersandeditors.com/major_writers_organizations_57410.htm) and Writer's Relief Writers Associations: Local And National Organizations For Writers (http://writersrelief.com/writers-associations-organizations/).

American Medical Writers Association (AMWA) (www.amwa.org/)

American Society of Journalists and Authors (ASJA) (www.asja.org)

Editorial Freelancers Association (EFA) (www.the-efa.org)

Florida Writers Association (FWA) (floridawriters.net)

Freelancers Union (www.freelancersunion.org/)

Gulf Coast Association of Creative Writing Teachers (GCACWT) (www.gcacwt.com/)

International Association of Business Communicators (IABC) (www.iabc.com/)

International Women's Writing Guild (iwwg.wildapricot.org/)

International Writers Association (IWA) (www. internationalwritersassociation.com/)

National Writers Union (NWU) (nwu.org/)

PEN America (pen.org/)

Professional Writers Association of Canada (pwac.ca/)

Public Relations Society of America, Inc. (PRSA) (www.prsa.org/)

Romance Writers of America (RWA) (www.rwanational.org)

Society of Professional Journalists (SPJ) (www.spj.org/)

Willamette Writers (willamettewriters.org/)

Tools, Apps and Other Resources

Relax Melodies—noise generation app (http://www. ipnossoft.com/)

myNoise.net—custom background noise machines and sound generator (mynoise.net/)

Poets&Writers.org's "The Time Is Now" writing prompts (www. pw.org/writing-prompts-exercises)

WritersDigest.com's "Creative Writing Prompts" (www. writersdigest.com/prompts)

ThinkWritten.com's "365 Creative Writing Prompts" (thinkwritten. com/365-creative-writing-prompts/)

Writing Prompts (writingprompts.tumblr.com/)

WritingForward.com (www.writingforward.com/category/ writing-prompts/fiction-writing-prompts)

CONTRIBUTORS

A heartfelt thank you to all those who have contributed their thoughts, suggestions and words of wisdom to this book. I couldn't have done it without you!

ACOSTA, CRISTINA

Artisanal design melds heart and place with art and craftsmanship. Designer and color expert Cristina Acosta stays connected to creative flow through painting and writing. She wrote *Paint Happy!* (North Light Press) and taught, designs home decor pieces and exhibits her art in galleries. Website: www.CristinaAcosta.com. Links: Facebook (www.facebook.com/Cristina.Acosta.artist), Instagram (www.instagram.com/cristinapacosta/), Twitter (twitter.com/cristinaacosta)

AMBERS, LORRAINE

Lorraine Ambers is a Welsh writer who lives in a pretty coastal town within Cardigan Bay. Her debut novel is YA fantasy romance and she is currently working on the second installment of the Shadow Knight series. Website: www.lorraineambers.com. Links: Facebook (www.facebook.com/AuthorLorraineAmbers/), Instagram (www.instagram.com/fantasywriter_lorraineambers), Twitter (mobile.twitter.com/LorraineAmbers)

ANGELL, HEIDI

Heidi Angell is a bibliophile, lexicomaniac and wordsmith. She is the author of *The Hunters Saga*, *The Clear Angel Chronicles*, *The Hell School Series*, *Royal Prince Vince*, *Creative Exercises to Inspire*, *The Penslinger's Ponderings*, and *The Survivalist Bible* series and *Dancing River Ranch* series, both releasing in 2017. Angell also heads up An Angell's Life of Bookish Goodness, a reading community she operates with her sons, which celebrates a love of reading. You can learn more at An Angell's Life of Bookish Goodness (www.patreon.com/bePatron?c=75268) Websites: www.heidiangell.com/. Links: Facebook (www.facebook.com/angellslife), Twitter (twitter.com/HeidiAngell), Instagram (www.instagram.com/heidiangellauthor/), Goodreads (www.goodreads.com/author/show/5139440.Heidi_Angell)

AVERBACH, PATRICIA

Patricia Averbach, a Cleveland native, is the former director of the Chautauqua Writers' Center in Chautauqua, New York. Her debut novel, *Painting Bridges* (Bottom Dog Press, 2013) was described by Michelle Ross, critic for the *Cleveland Plain Dealer*, as intelligent, introspective and moving. Her poetry chapbook, *Missing Persons* (Ward Wood Publishing, 2013) received the London-based Lumen/Camden prize in 2013 and was listed by *Times of London Literary Supplement* (November 14, 2014) as one of the best short collections of the year. Website: patriciaaverbach.com

BARKAN, JOSH

Josh Barkan has won the Lightship International Short Story Prize and has been a finalist for the Grace Paley Prize for Short Fiction, the Paterson Fiction Prize, and the Juniper Prize for Fiction. He is the recipient of a fellowship from the National Endowment for the Arts, and his writing has appeared in *Esquire*. He earned his MFA from the Iowa Writers' Workshop and has taught writing at Harvard, Boston University, and New York University. His books include *Mexico: Stories*, *Blind Speed: A Novel*, and *Before*

Hiroshima. With his wife, a painter from Mexico, he divides his time between Mexico City and Roanoke, Virginia. Website: www.joshbarkan.com

BARRETT, LYNNE

Lynne Barrett's *What Editors Want: A Must-Read for Writers Submitting to Literary Magazines* is out from Rain Chain Press. Her story collection *Magpies* won the Florida Book Awards gold medal for fiction, and her recent work can be found in *Necessary Fiction, Mystery Tribune, Fort Lauderdale Magazine, The Southern Women's Review, One Year to a Writing Life*, and other anthologies and magazines. She edits *The Florida Book Review* and teaches at Florida International University. Website: www.lynnebarrett.com. Links: Twitter (twitter.com/LynneBarrett), Facebook (www.facebook.com/LynneBarrettauthor/)

BAUM, ROBIN

Robin Baum has been an independent writer, editor, and media relations professional since 2013. She has acquired more than a quarter century of experience in various aspects of corporate, non-profit, personal and literary writing, editing and media relations, including 13 years as a healthcare industry writer for a global medical device manufacturer and 26 years writing and editing for healthcare start-ups, small businesses, sole proprietors and non-profit organizations in Ohio and around the country. Her current active nonprofit commitments include assisting the CEO of the Lakeland Foundation at Lakeland Community College with special projects and serving as Communication Committee chair for the Lake Health Foundation Board of Trustees. She holds a bachelor of arts in psychology from the University of California at Los Angeles (UCLA) and a certificate in business management from Lakeland Community College. Links: LinkedIn (www.linkedin.com/pub/robin-baum/7/527/356)

BECK, JAMIE

National best-selling author Jamie Beck's realistic and heartwarming stories have sold more than one million copies. A 2017 Booksellers' Best Award finalist, her books have also hit Heavy.com's Top 10 Romance Novels of 2015 and been selected as a Woman's World Book Club pick. Critics at *Kirkus, Publisher's Weekly* (including a starred review), and *Booklist* have alternatively called her work "smart," "uplifting," and "entertaining." In addition to writing novels, she enjoys dancing around the kitchen while cooking and hitting the slopes in Vermont and Utah. Above all, she is a grateful wife and mother to a very patient, supportive family. Website: www.jamiebeck.com. Links: Facebook (www.facebook.com/jamiebeckbooks), Twitter (www.twitter.com/writerjamiebeck), Instagram (www.instagram.com/writerjamiebeck), Pinterest (www.pinterest.com/writerjamiebeck), Goodreads (www.goodreads.com/author/show/8020971.Jamie_Beck)

CILETTI, MARIA

Author Maria V. Ciletti is a registered nurse and is currently working as a medical administrator for a family practice in Niles, Ohio. Her first novel, *The Choice* (a 2007 Lambda Literary nominee for debut fiction), was published by Haworth Press in May 2007. *Clinical Distance*, the sequel to *The Choice; Will You Still Love Me Tomorrow* (the third book in the *Choice* series); *Entangled*, a stand-alone controversial romance; and *Collide* (Golden Crown Literary Society finalist for best romance in 2011) were all published by Intaglio Publications. Her nonfiction credits include Living Now Book Award winner *I Have to Leave You Now: A Survival Guide for Caregivers of Loved Ones with Alzheimer's Disease* and its companion book, *Taking Care: A Caregivers Guide for Navigating the Health Care System* (published in 2015 by Dragonfly Publications). She lives in Niles, Ohio, with her partner Rose. Website: www.mariaciletti.com. Links: Facebook (www.facebook.com/maria.ciletti).

DUKE, PAIGE

Paige Duke is an independent editor helping authors to polish their work, grow their writing craft, and get their books into the hands of adoring fans. Website: www.thepaigeduke.com.

FELIX, GILLIAN

Novelist and scriptwriter Gillian Felix has been writing since she was old enough to hold a pencil. She enjoys creating characters that could be your next-door neighbor, but would you want them as your neighbor is another story. Originally from Trinidad and Tobago, the island country of the southeastern West Indies, Felix moved to the United States in 1998 and since then has been involved in the entertainment industry. She is trained in the Meisner and Stanislavski technique of acting, which she credits as an asset to her character development and writing. An entrepreneur and advocate for children's and women's rights, Felix volunteers at the New Mexico Children's Grief Center. Websites: www.plaintalkbm.com/, www.plaintalkbm.com/family-portrait-novel. Links: Facebook fan page (www.facebook.com/FamilyPortraitNovels), Twitter (www.twitter.com/gillianfx), LinkedIn (www.linkedin.com/in/gillianfelix), Goodreads (www.goodreads.com/author/show/7210783.Gillian_Felix), Google+ (plus.google.com/u/0/+GillianFelix/posts)

FREEMAN, KERIN

Kerin Freeman is an editor/proofreader of long standing. She has two books published, one a biography of an adventurous, courageous, intelligent George Cross medal holder, *The Civilian Bomb Disposing Earl*, plus a novel about a young soldier set in England and France during WWII, *War and Chance*. She is now working on two manuscripts: a novel on time travel set in 1980s and 1940s England, and a novel based on a true story, *Murder in the Milkbar*, set in New Zealand in the 1950s. Website: kerinfreeman.webs.com/. Links: Facebook (www.facebook.com/kerin.freeman), Twitter (twitter.com/freelancerkerf)

GORMAN, ANITA

Anita G. Gorman grew up in New York City and is aging in northeast Ohio. Her scholarly work has appeared in such publications as *Clues: A Journal of Detection, FOLLY, Mythlore, Dime Novel Roundup*, the *Swedish-American Historical Quarterly*, and in nine volumes of the *Dictionary of Literary Biography*. "Where Are You, O High-School Friends?" was published in *Unfinished Chapters* (2015) and "Finding Bill" in *Finding Mr. Right* (2016). Her short stories have appeared in *Gilbert, Down in the Dirt, Dual Coast, Jitter Press, Knee-Jerk*, and *Speculative Grammarian*

GROTH, TARA LYNNE

Tara Lynne Groth writes short fiction and poetry. Her work has appeared in multiple journals, and one of her poems was selected to inspire two community art sculptures in 2014. She received honorable mention in fiction in the 2015 Carolina Woman Writing Contest and was a semifinalist for the 2015 and 2016 James Applewhite Poetry Prize. She is an alumna of the Southampton Writers Conference. Websites: www.taralynnegroth.com, www.writenaked.net. Links: LinkedIn (www.linkedin.com/in/0taralynne/), YouTube (www.youtube.com/user/taralynnegroth), Google+ (plus.google.com/u/0/110240790560319164872)

GURVIS, SANDRA

Sandra Gurvis is the author of hundreds of magazine articles and sixteen commercially published books, including *Country Club Wives*, a novel optioned for TV by Insight Productions. Her most recent nonfiction project is *Close Enough For Government Work: America's Presidential Libraries*. Websites: www.sandragurvis.com, www.booksaboutthe60s.com. Links: Facebook (www.facebook.com/Country-Club-Wives-103644326397112/, www.facebook.com/POTUShouse)

HENRY, ANN

Ann Henry is the award-winning author of *The Novel Pitch: Everything You Need to Know to Write a Successful Query for Your Fiction* as well as the novels *A Bit of Sun* and *Sailing Away from the Moon*. She serves as copy editor and pitch writer for Ann Henry Literary Services, which also offers interior book design, book formatting, and book cover design at www.AnnHenry.com. Check out her Know Your Words, Weekly Pitch, and Literary License blogs at www.ProseAct.com. Websites: www.AnnHenry. com, www.ProseAct.com

JANES, WENDY

As a freelance proofreader and editor, Wendy Janes works with publishers and individual authors. She is also a caseworker for The National Autistic Society's Education Rights Service. Author of short stories and the novel *What Jennifer Knows*, she loves to take real life and turn it into fiction. She lives in London with her husband and youngest son. Website: wendyproof.co.uk/. Links: Facebook author page (www.facebook.com/Wendy-Janes-976051022455216), Twitter (twitter.com/wendyproof), Amazon author pages (UK/US) (www.amazon.co.uk/-/e/ B016J66C9G)

JENKINS, SHARON C.

Sharon is the Inspirational Principal for The Master Communicator's Writing Services, providing writing and coaching services to small businesses and authors. Known as The Master Communicator, Sharon is proficient in communicating in all forms of media: radio, newspapers, magazines, and spoken word. A best-selling and award-winning author whose titles include *Authorpreneurship: The Business Start-Up Manual for Authors*, her most recent e-book release is the *Periscope Your Book Series Book Three, Using Periscope to #CreateBookBuzz*. She is currently working on a book titled *Christian Authorpreneurship, Mastering the Business of Writing*, which has an anticipated December 2017 release. Website: www.

sharoncjenkins.com. Links: Facebook (www.facebook.com/ SharoncJenkins, www.facebook.com/mcwritingservices, www. facebook.com/authorpreneurship), Twitter (twitter.com/Sharon_ Jenkins), LinkedIn (www.linkedin.com/in/sharoncjenkins), Instagram (instagram.com/sharoncjenkins)

KARL, ALLAN

Allan Karl is an author, photographer, professional keynote speaker, committed adventurer, and digital marketing strategist. With an insatiable passion for travel, culture, people, and food, he has explored more than 60 countries all over the world, photographing, writing, and blogging about them along the way. In his best-selling book, *FORKS: A Quest for Culture, Cuisine, and Connection*, Karl brings to life his three-year solo journey around the world on a motorcycle. When not traveling the world, Allan serves as principal of WorldRider Productions where he focuses on speaking, publishing, coaching, and creating content that brings to life his stories and experiences around the world— demonstrating again and again how the discoveries he has made and the lessons learned can help all of us lead more rewarding lives. Websites: www.worldrider.com, www.allankarl.com, www. forksthebook.com, www.digitaltavern.com

KELLY, CAITLIN

Caitlin Kelly frequently writes for the *New York Times* where she has published more than 50 stories, several the most-read of the day's edition. Winner of a Canadian National Magazine Award, she is a former reporter for *The Globe and Mail, Montreal Gazette* and *New York Daily News*. Her blog, www.broadside-blog.wordpress.com, has 17,306 readers worldwide. Author of *Malled: My Unintentional Career in Retail* and *Blown Away: American Women and Guns*, she lives in Tarrytown, NY. She is a graduate of the University of Toronto. Websites: caitlinkelly.com/, www.broadsideblog.wordpress.com. Links: Twitter (twitter.com/ caitlinkellynyc)

KINCER, LAURIE

Laurie Kincer, Writers' Center Specialist at Cuyahoga County Public Library near Cleveland, Ohio, coordinates the new William N. Skirball Writers' Center at the South Euclid-Lyndhurst Branch of CCPL, offering free writing workshops, conferences, and author visits. She has presented on "Libraries Influence Readers, Writers and Communities" at the annual conference of the Association of Writers and Writing Programs. With an MA in English from Case Western Reserve University and an MLIS from Kent State University, she has served as a children's, teen, and adult librarian in public libraries since 1998.

KLEIN, CHRISTOPHER

Christopher Klein is a Boston-based author and freelance writer specializing in history, travel, and sports. He is the author of *Strong Boy: The Life and Times of John L. Sullivan, America's First Sports Hero* (Lyons Press, 2013), *The Die-Hard Sports Fan's Guide to Boston* (Union Park Press, 2009) and *Discovering the Boston Harbor Islands: A Guide to the City's Hidden Shores* (Union Park Press, 2008). A frequent contributor to the *Boston Globe* and History.com, Klein has also written for the *New York Times, National Geographic Traveler, Harvard Magazine, Red Sox Magazine*, ESPN.com, Smithsonian. com and AmericanHeritage.com. Website: www.christopherklein. com/. Links: Twitter (www.twitter.com/historyauthor), Facebook (www.facebook.com/authorchristopherklein)

LANGLEY, DAWN RENO

Dawn Reno Langley is a writer, theater critic, mosaic artist, and educator who has devoted her life to literature and the arts. She has written extensively for newspapers and magazines, has published more than 30 books (children's, adult novels, and nonfiction), and has published award-winning short stories, essays, and poetry as well as theater reviews and blogs. A Fulbright scholar with an MFA in Fiction and a PhD in Interdisciplinary Studies, Langley lives in Durham, North Carolina, a small city where

people present her with new stories every day. Website: www.
dawnrenolangley.com. Links: Twitter (twitter.com/proflangley)

LAVENDER, MARIE
Best-selling and award-winning author Marie Lavender has
published 22 books in the genres of historical romance,
contemporary romance, romantic suspense, paranormal
romance, fantasy, science fiction, mystery/thriller, dramatic
fiction, literary fiction and poetry. She has also contributed to
several multi-author anthologies. Her current series are *The
Heiresses in Love Series*, *The Magick Series*, *The Blood at First Sight
Series* and *The Code of Endhivar Series*. Websites: marielavender.
com/, iloveromanceblog.wordpress.com/, marielavenderbooks.
blogspot.com/, marielavender.blogspot.com/. Links: Facebook
(www.facebook.com/marie.lavender.58, www.facebook.com/
MarieAnnLavender), Twitter (twitter.com/marielavender1),
Amazon author page (Author.to/MarieLavender)

LEIGH, VICKI
Adopted at three days old by a construction worker and a stay-
at-home mom, Vicki Leigh grew up in a small suburb of Akron,
Ohio, where she learned to read by the age of four and considered
being sent to her room for punishment as an opportunity to dive
into another book. By the sixth grade, Leigh penned her first, full-
length screenplay. If she couldn't be a writer, Leigh would be a
Hunter (think Dean and Sam Winchester) or a Jedi. Her favorite
place on earth is Hogwarts (she refuses to believe it doesn't exist),
and her favorite dreams include solving cases alongside Sherlock
Holmes. She also writes YA Contemporary as Tori Rigby. Website:
www.vickitoriwrites.com. Links: Twitter (www.twitter.com/
vickitoriwrites), Facebook (www.facebook.com/vickitoriwrites),
Instagram (www.instagram.com/vickitoriwrites)

LIAO, KIM

Kim Liao's work has appeared in *Salon, Lit Hub, The Rumpus, River Teeth, Vol. 1 Brooklyn, Another Chicago Magazine, Fourth River, Fringe*, and others. A former Fulbright Taiwan Creative Research Scholar, she is currently finishing her first novel and revising a family memoir about the Taiwanese Independence Movement. Links: Twitter (twitter.com/the_kimlet)

LINDSEY, JULIE ANNE

Julie Anne Lindsey is a multi-genre author who writes the stories that keep her up at night. A self-proclaimed nerd with a penchant for words and proclivity for fun, Lindsey lives in Ohio with her husband and three spunky children. Today, she hopes to make someone smile. One day she plans to change the world. She is a member of the International Thriller Writers (ITW), Romance Writers of America (RWA), and Sisters in Crime (SinC), and is represented by Jill Marsal of Marsal Lyon Literary Agency. Lindsey also writes as Julie Chase. Websites: www.julieannelindsey.com, www.juliechasebooks.com/. Links: Twitter (twitter.com/JulieALindsey), Facebook (facebook.com/JulieAnneLindseyAuthor), Pinterest (pinterest.com/juliealindsey)

LOREN, RONI

Roni Loren wrote her first romance novel at age fifteen when she discovered writing about boys was way easier than actually talking to them. Since then, her flirting skills haven't improved, but she likes to think her storytelling ability has. If she's not working on her latest sexy story, you can find her cooking, watching reality television, or picking up another hobby she doesn't need—in other words, procrastinating like a boss. She is a RITA Award winner and a *New York Times* and *USA Today* best-selling author. Website: www.roniloren.com. Links: Twitter (www.twitter.com/roniloren), Facebook (www.facebook.com/roniloren), Instagram (www.instagram.com/roniloren)

MARTIN, MANJULA

Manjula Martin is the editor of the anthology *Scratch: Writers, Money, and the Art of Making a Living* (Simon & Schuster, 2017). She has written for numerous publications, including the *Virginia Quarterly Review* and *Pacific Standard*, and she is the managing editor of *Zoetrope: All-Story*. Website: manjulamartin.com/. Three Cents Newsletter: tinyletter.com/3cents

MARTINEZ, ROD

Rod Martinez was born and raised in Tampa, Florida, and was attracted to words at an early age. His first book, *The Boy Who Liked To Read*, was created in grade school; his teacher used it to encourage creativity in her students. Eventually he discovered comic books, but his high school English teacher told him to try short story writing. Martinez, the recipient of the 2017 Jerry Spinelli Scholarship from the Highlights Foundation, wrote a middle-grade adventure, *The Juniors*, that was picked up by a publisher, and the rest, as they say, is history. Website: www.rodmartinez.us. Links: Facebook (www.facebook.com/authorrodmartinez)

MICHAELS, CAT

Author and blogger Cat Michaels, MS, Ed., has more than two decades of experience helping students from kindergarten to college with learning disabilities and Asperger's syndrome. Her chapter books and Sweet T Tales series for beginning readers tell of everyday life with a twist of magic and mischief. Michael's books encourage young and reluctant readers to use their imagination and solve kid-sized dilemmas as they enjoy reading. Michaels lives in North Carolina with her family, where she enjoys digital photography and graphic design, creates pocket gardens, works out as often as she can, and writes. Website: www. catmichaelswriter.com. Links: Facebook (www. facebook.com/catmichaelswriter), Twitter (www.twitter.com/ catmichaelsbook), Pinterest (www.pinterest.com/catmichaels), Instagram (www.instagram.com/catmichaels.writer/), Amazon

(www.amazon.com/Cat-Michaels/e/B00GEAJQTQ),
iTunes (itunes.apple.com/us/author/cat-michaels/
id1173086551?mt=11)

ORENSTEIN, FRAN
Fran Orenstein, EdD, award-winning author and poet, wrote her
first poem at age eight and submitted a short story to a magazine
at age twelve. She wrote professionally and academically until she
retired and began to write a variety of fiction and poetry. Her publications include a collection of adult paranormal short stories, a
historical murder mystery romance, and a contemporary mystery
romance as well as young-adult and children's books. Orenstein
has a BA in Early Childhood Education, MEd in Counseling
Psychology, and EdD in Child and Youth Studies. She has been a
member of The National League of American Pen Women, Sisters
in Crime, The Society of Children's Book Writers and Illustrators,
and statewide authors' and poets' groups in Arizona and Florida.
Orenstein now resides in the Atlanta, Georgia, area. Website:
www.franorenstein.com. Links: Facebook (www.facebook.com/
profile.php?id=1253621499), LinkedIn (www.linkedin.com/
pub/dr-fran-orenstein/1b/278/295), Twitter (twitter.com/
Hubysmom), Amazon (www.amazon.com/Fran-Orenstein/e/
B004ILD540)

PEARCE, Q.L.
Q.L. Pearce is a multi-genre author who has written nearly two
hundred books: educational, craft, nonfiction, biography, and
fiction. Pearce lives in southern California with her husband,
William, a physiologist; two beautiful dogs, Lucia the Weimaraner
and Sasha the Norwegian Elkhound; a quirky cockatiel named
Buddy who will tell anyone within hearing that he is a very good
boy; and a bevy of fish. When not writing, she loves to read,
garden, and of course, travel. Website: www.qlpearce.com/. Links:
Twitter (twitter.com/qlpearce), YouTube (www.youtube.com/
watch?v=db4aQLSyKMg&feature=youtu.be), Goodreads (www.

goodreads.com/author/show/5659856.Q_L_Pearce), LinkedIn (www.linkedin.com/in/q-l-pearce-7926604), Facebook (www.facebook.com/ql.pearce)

PECK, LISA
Lisa Peck, ASID, owner of LiLu Interiors, prides herself on creating environments that align with and support her clients' core values for their lives at home and work. During her 30 years in the industry, Peck has collaborated with a host of people on a variety of projects that span the gamut of style. A master with color, Peck is an expert at working within three-dimensional space, identifying hard materials and mixing them with textures and patterns. Her work has been published locally and nationally in design magazines and books. Websites: www.liluinteriors.com, www.sylvieandmira.com. Links: LinkedIn (www.linkedin.com/in/lisapeck), Instagram (www.instagram.com/lilumpls), Facebook (www.facebook.com/LiLuInteriors)

PENN, JOANNA
Joanna Penn is a *New York Times* and *USA Today* best-selling author of thrillers under J.F. Penn. She also writes inspirational nonfiction for authors and is an award-winning creative entrepreneur and international professional speaker. Her site, TheCreativePenn.com, is regularly voted one of the top 10 sites for writers and self-publishers. Websites: www.thecreativepenn.com/, www.JFPenn.com. Links: Twitter (twitter.com/thecreativepenn), Facebook (Facebook.com/TheCreativePenn, Facebook.com/JFPennAuthor [for fiction]), Instagram (Instagram/JFPennAuthor), Google+ (GooglePlus/JoannaPenn), LinkedIn (LinkedIn/joannapenn)

PIGEON, STÉPHANE, PhD
Stéphane Pigeon received the degree of electrical engineering from the Université Catholique de Louvain (UCL) in June 1994, with a specialization in signal processing, and his PhD in Applied Science from the Université Catholique de Louvain. Pigeon devotes most

of his time developing myNoise.net, the premier online noise generator, as well as working as a consultant. He is open to collaborations in the field of audio processing, with sound processing for healthcare applications representing one of his recent favorite topics. And his heart still belongs to the programming of sounds for electronic music instruments. Website: stephanepigeon.com

PROTZMAN, CLIFF

Cliff Protzman was a winner in the 2015 real-life writing contest, *Unfinished Chapters*. His essay, "Three Words," features the relationship with his father and a baseball hero. His debut novel, *Dead Air*, a murder mystery was published September 2017. A graduate of the University of Pittsburgh, Cliff is a member of the Mystery Writers of America and Pennwriters. Website: www. cliffprotzman.com

QUIGLEY, TIMOTHY

Timothy Quigley's award-winning stories have appeared in the *Chariton Review, Line Zero Journal of Art and Literature, La Ostra Magazine* and *Writer's World* as well as online publications. He is a scriptwriter for Convergence Design and is currently working on two short films: one animated, and the other a live action adapted from his short fiction. His novella, *Kissing the Hag*, was released by Pixel Hall Press in 2015. He lives in Salem, Massachusetts, and teaches writing at Salem State University and Wentworth Institute in Boston. Website: www.timothyquigley.org

RAFTER, MICHELLE V.

Michelle V. Rafter is a business journalist covering jobs, workplace issues, transportation, and how tech is transforming them all. She's a regular contributor to *Workforce*, TalentEconomy.io, Trucks. com, Best Lawyers, Great Place to Work, Boston Consulting Group and *San Diego Union-Tribune*, among others. She lives in Portland, Oregon, home of big trees, #TrailBlazers, and good beer. Website: michellerafter.com/. Links: Twitter (twitter.com/MichelleRafter), LinkedIn (www.linkedin.com/in/michellerafter/)

RELPH, MRIDU KHULLAR
Mridu Khullar Relph is the founder of The International Freelancer. She has written for the *New York Times*, *TIME*, *CNN*, *ABC*, *Christian Science Monitor*, *Ms.*, *Marie Claire*, and many more in a career spanning over 15 years. Website: www.TheInternationalFreelancer.com. Links: Twitter (twitter.com/mridukhullar), Facebook (www.facebook.com/MriduKhullarRelph), Google+ (plus.google.com/+MriduKhullarRelph), Pinterest (www.pinterest.com/mridukhullar/), Stumble (www.stumbleupon.com/stumbler/mridukhullar)

ROUTEN, BARBARA
Barbara Routen, a former *Tampa Tribune* columnist and correspondent, loves writing articles that inform, encourage, and inspire. She is a FOCUS-Plant City staff writer and columnist, a National League of American Pen Women member and *Chicken Soup for the Soul* and *The Pen Woman Magazine* contributor. Contact her at Barbara.Routen@gmail.com. Links: Google+ (plus.google.com/u/0/103546841862237184382), Twitter (twitter.com/BarbaraRouten), LinkedIn (www.linkedin.com/in/barbararouten/)

SAGERT, KELLY BOYER
Kelly Boyer Sagert is the writer/researcher of the 2017 Emmy-nominated documentary, *Trail Magic: The Grandma Gatewood Story* (www.edenvalleyenterprises.org/progdesc/gatewood/gtwdinf.htm). She has written four full-length commissioned plays and traditionally published 14 books, along with thousands of articles. She previously worked as a magazine editor and speaks at writers' conferences in the Midwest and at the American Society of Journalists and Authors conference in New York City. She has taught writing online for *Writer's*

Digest since 2000. Websites: www.kbsagert.com and www. everythingtogodinprayer.com. Links: Facebook (www.facebook. com/kbsagert), Twitter: (www.twitter.com/kbsagert), LinkedIn (www.linkedin.com/in/kellyboyersagert/), Google+ (plus.google. com/u/0/+KellyBoyerSagert)

SCHWARTZ, DIANNE
Dianne Schwartz has been an advocate for battered women since 1990 and founded Educating Against Domestic Violence. Her book, *Whose Face Is in the Mirror?* was chosen as the Hay Foundation Book of the Year. She is also a Licensed Esthetician and a Hospice volunteer. Links: Facebook (www. facebook.com/dianne.penningtonschwartz), Amazon Author Page (www.amazon.com/Dianne-Schwartz/e/B001K8NNC8/ ref=dp_byline_cont_book_1)

SOFFER, JESSICA
Jessica Soffer earned her MFA at Hunter College. A Hertog Fellow and recipient of the Bernard Cohen Prize, her work has appeared in *Granta,* the *New York Times, Martha Stewart Living, Real Simple, Redbook, Saveur, The Wall Street Journal, Vogue,* and on NPR's Selected Shorts. Her debut novel, *Tomorrow There Will Be Apricots,* was published in twelve countries. Website: www.jessicasoffer.com/

SOUTHARD, SCOTT D.
Scott D. Southard is the author of *A Jane Austen Daydream* and *Permanent Spring Showers.* He can be followed at "The Musings &Artful Blunders of Scott D. Southard" at sdsouthard.com and @ sdsouthard via Twitter. Website: sdsouthard.com/. Links: Twitter (twitter.com/SDSouthard), Facebook (www.facebook.com/ ScottDSouthard)

STRAWSER, JESSICA

Jessica Strawser is the editorial director of *Writer's Digest* magazine and the author of *Almost Missed You*, named to Barnes & Noble's Best New Fiction shortlist for March 2017, PopSugar's Best Spring Reads, and BookBub's "17 Breakthrough Books of Spring 2017." She has written for the *New York Times'* "Modern Love" column, *Publishers Weekly* and other fine venues and lives with her husband and two children in Cincinnati, Ohio. Website: jessicastrawser.com. Links: Facebook (www.Facebook.com/jessicastrawserauthor), Twitter (www.twitter.com/jessicastrawser)

SUTRO, MARIE

Marie Sutro is the author of *Dark Associations*, a fast-paced psychological thriller set in the San Francisco Bay Area about SFPD Detective Kate Barnes' quest to stop one of the most insidious serial killers of all time. Sutro is a member of the acclaimed mystery writers' organization, Sisters in Crime, and volunteers with California Library Literacy Services, helping adults improve their reading and writing skills. Web site: www.mariesutro.com/. Links: Facebook (www.facebook.com/MarieSutro/), Twitter (twitter.com/mariesutro), Instagram (www.instagram.com/mariesutro/)

TALLER, CLAUDIA J.

Claudia J. Taller is a writer, artist, yoga instructor, and initiator from Northeast Ohio who writes travel, history, and lifestyle articles for local and national publications, has several books to her credit, and stages creativity and spiritual events. Prior to earning a bachelor's degree in English and a Writing Certificate from Kent State University, she interned with the Kent State University Press, served as editor of the campus literary magazine, and worked with the faculty on the creation of the University's Writing Certificate Program. Website: www.claudiajtaller.com/

TICE, CAROL

Carol Tice is the author of ten books covering writing and small business and, since 2005, has been a full-time freelancer for both publications and businesses with a client list that includes *Forbes, Entrepreneur* and *The Writer's Market* to Costco and American Express. She also writes the Make a Living Writing blog, where she teaches freelance writers how to grow their income, and created the membership community Freelance Writers Den. Websites: www.caroltice.com, freelancewritersden.com/, www.makealiving-writing.com/. Links: Twitter (twitter.com/ticewrites), LinkedIn (www.linkedin.com/in/caroltice/), Facebook (www.facebook.com/makealivingwriting), Google+ (plus.google.com/+CarolTice)

WALD, CATHERINE

Catherine Wald is a NYC-based author, journalist, poet and teacher who continues to collect numerous rejections and is also occasionally published. For more, visit her website, explore her books (*The Resilient Writer, Distant, burned-out stars, Childish Things*) or watch her read an essay about post-Trump bra-buying. Website: www.catherinewald.com/

WEINBLATT, CHARLES

Charles S. Weinblatt was born in Toledo, Ohio, in 1952. He is a retired University of Toledo administrator and a published author. His biography appears in Wikipedia and Marquis Who's Who in America. Weinblatt is a reviewer for the *New York Journal of Books*. Websites: charlesweinblatt.wix.com/charles-s-weinblatt, www.smashwords.com/profile/view/cweinblatt. Links: Twitter (twitter.com/Chuck_Weinblatt), Facebook (www.facebook.com/jacobs.courage), YouTube (youtu.be/GHqowym6wyU)

WOOD, WALLY

Wally Wood has published three novels, *Getting Oriented: A Novel about Japan, The Girl in the Photo* and *Death in a Family Business*. As a ghostwriter, his credits include 21 nonfiction business books.

He is currently writing his fourth novel and translating a collection of Japanese short stories into English. He obtained his MA in creative writing in 2002 from the City University of New York. Website: mysteriesofwriting.blogspot.com/. Links: Facebook (www.facebook.com/wal.wood.3), LinkedIn (www.linkedin.com/in/wallywood)

ABOUT THE AUTHOR

Nancy Christie has been writing since second grade—she would have started sooner but she had to learn how to print first—and, except for some "life intermissions," hasn't stopped since.

A writer by profession and preference, Christie began her writing career working for newspapers and magazines, and then branched out into copywriting for companies and ad agencies. Her articles, fiction and essays have appeared in numerous print and online publications.

Along the way, Christie authored the inspirational book *The Gifts of Change*, the literary fiction collection *Traveling Left of Center and Other Stories*, and two short fiction e-books: *Annabelle* and *Alice in Wonderland*. *Rut-Busting Book for Writers*, her most recent book, provides tips and strategies to help writers break out of the writing rut and move toward their professional or creative goals.

Christie is also a speaker on writing and self-motivation topics, whose presentations include her popular "Rut-Busting" series of workshops.

The founder of "Celebrate Short Fiction" Day, an annual celebration of short stories and those who write them, Christie is a member of the American Society of Journalists and Authors (ASJA), Short Fiction Writers Guild (SFWG), and the Florida Writers Association (FWA).

For more information, visit her website at www.nancychristie. com, her Goodreads page (www.goodreads.com/NancyChristie) and her Amazon Author page (www.amazon.com/author/ nancychristie).

You can also follow her on social media:

- Twitter (@NChristie_OH)

- Facebook (www.facebook.com/NancyChristieAuthor/)

- LinkedIn (www.linkedin.com/in/nancychristie/)

- Google+ (https://plus.google.com/+NancyChristiewriter/)

Books by Nancy Christie

Rut-Busting Book for Writers (Mill City Press)—www.rutbusting-bookforwriters.com/

Traveling Left of Center and Other Stories (Pixel Hall Press)—www. travelingleftofcenter.com/

Annabelle (Pixel Hall Press)—www.nancychristie.com/books/ annabelle/

Alice in Wonderland (Pixel Hall Press)—www.nancychristie.com/books/alice/

The Gifts of Change (Atria/Beyond Words)—www.giftsof-change.com/

Contact Nancy Christie

To request an interview or schedule an appearance or workshop by Nancy Christie for your event or organization, contact her via phone or email.
Nancy Christie
PO Box 4505, Austintown, OH 44515
330-793-3675
nancy@nancychristie.com
www.nancychristie.com

CPSIA information can be obtained
at www.ICGtesting.com
Printed in the USA
LVHW03s2140180618
581184LV00001B/52/P